Don

Donkeys as pets

Donkey Keeping, Care, Pros and Cons, Housing, Diet and Health.

by

Roger Rodendale

Table of Contents

Introduction

One of the most unusual choices for a pet is a donkey. Yet unknown to most people, a donkey can make for a very loyal and intelligent pet. These creatures are extremely gentle and have a very peaceful quality about them. When you look into the eyes of a donkey you will see nothing but gentleness.

However, let that not be the only reason why you bring a donkey home as a pet. They are adorable but require a lot of work and dedication from the owners.

When you decide to bring a donkey home as a pet, there are several things that you need to consider, the main thing being the availability of space for your new pet. They are not animals that can be kept in small areas. They need a dedicated space that can be used when you want them to rest or just stay in.

Donkeys are known to love being around people when they are accustomed to it. A lot of pet owners prefer a donkey because they can perform tasks like carrying all your tools if you are working in the garden, follow you on a trail and even just cuddle with you.

They are great around kids as long as you are able to tell your children how to interact with the animal correctly. They make great companions, especially if you have a stable with a lonely horse. Yes, horses and donkeys make great companions.

Donkeys are extremely emotional and sensitive as well. These creatures will actually mourn the death of someone close with a very typical bray. They love to play and are quite bright. So if you look at the low-key demeanor of a donkey, make sure that you don't let that fool you into believing that the donkey is a dull animal.

Since these pets are quite unusual, you are likely to find less information about owning these animals from other pet owners. That is why this book brings to you a lot of practical knowledge through extensive research. It is a compilation of information from donkey owners to make sure that you have tips that you can actually put to use.

The book contains everything that you need to know from the types of donkeys that you can bring home, introducing a donkey into your household, training them, feeding them, housing them and also ensuring that they are always in good health.

4

The idea is to give you a step-by-step process of getting used to a donkey as a pet. You see, unlike a conventional pet like a dog or a cat, most people do not know what to expect from a donkey. If this book is able to give you that insight, then you are sure to have a great time with your new pet.

Before you decide to commit to a donkey, make sure that you amass as much information as you can to ensure that you have the resources, the time and the finances to take care of one.

Chapter 1: Learning about donkeys

The donkey, in popular perception, is a dim-witted creature whose only purpose is to carry a load on his back. But, if you move away from this popular perception, you will see that they are delightful creatures that actually make great pets.

Donkeys were among the first animals to be domesticated and have been around humans for as long as you can imagine. So, it is quite natural for them to be able to live among us peacefully and even become great companions over time. In this chapter we will talk about the history and origin of this rather magnificent species.

1. History of domestication

The earliest reference to donkeys was as food, so it is possible that they were hunted, based on the Egyptian murals that were found in the tomb of Pharaoh Tutankhamun. These illustrations show some elite nobles engaging in a wild ass hunt.

About 6000 years ago, the donkey as we know it today was bred from the wild ass in Africa. This was during the predynastic era in Egypt. It is believed the two sub species of the wild ass were used to develop the modern donkey. They were the *Equusafricanusafricanus*or the Nubian ass and the *Equusafricanussomalinsis.* Both these species are still alive but are currently listed under the IUCN Red List.

The importance of the donkey actually came to the forefront as its role as a pack animal. These animals were adapted to live in the desert and were also great for carrying loads and moving them across long distances with their herd. In the continents of Asia and Africa, especially, the donkey played an important role in transporting food and goods for trade.

a. Archeological proof of evolution

There is a lot of archeological evidence that suggests that there have been many changes in the body of the donkey that was domesticated over the years. This body morphology has made them quite different from the donkeys that they are believed to have originated from.

Domestic donkeys are much smaller in size. Their metacarpals or the bones in their feet are smaller than and not as robust as the wild ancestors.

The evidence of proper burial sites for donkeys suggests that they were trusted animals that served an important purpose domestically. There is a lot of pathological evidence to suggest that these animals also went through a lot of damage to their spinal cord. This shows that they must have been used to carry heavy loads on their backs. This was not the case with their ancestors.

The earliest evidence of the buried bones of the domesticated donkey dates back to 4000-4600 BC. These bones were unearthed from a predynastic Maadi site near Cairo in a site that was called El-Omari. In fact, special tombs were made to bury the donkey. These "cemeteries" were found in areas like Tarkhan, Abydos and other predynastic sites. Other areas where these bones were found are Iran, Iraq and Syria. These bones date back to 2800 BC. Another well-known site is the UanMuhuggiag in Libya. The samples from this region are almost 3000 years old and probably the oldest.

b. Samples at Abydos
In the year 2008, a study revealed the skeleton of 10 donkeys at the predynastic archaeological site at Abydos. It was seen that these tombs were made of bricks and were actually adjacent to the tomb of an Egyptian King. While there were no grave goods in these tombs, it was confirmed that these were the skeletons of donkeys.

The vertebral bones showed a lot of strain, which shows clearly that even back then these were beasts of burden. The morphology of the body was somewhere half way between the modern donkey and the wild ass. This has led to a lot of debate about whether these creatures were fully domesticated in that period or not. It is possible that they were not fully domesticated as they are today.

c. The DNA of the donkey
The sequencing of the ancient DNA of the historic, ancient and modern excavations of these donkey fossils in the northeastern part of Africa suggest that the modern donkey has solely evolved from the wild Nubian ass. These excavations were as recent as 2010 and include sites like UanMuhuggiag in Libya.

The DNA sequence in the mitochondria of the Somali and Nubian wild ass is very distinct. So, when you compare it with the DNA sequence of the ancient domestic donkey, it is more related to the Nubian Wild ass. So, it seems like the modern wild Nubian ass is actually a descendant of the modern donkey!

Cattle herders have domesticated wild asses for years now. The earliest records of these animals go all the way back to 8900-8400 years ago. When interbreeding between the domestic ass and the wild ass took place, it continued throughout this process of domestication. In the Bronze Age, however, the Egyptian asses showed more morphological resemblance to the wild varieties. This suggested that the process of domestication was either really long and slow or that there were some characteristics in the wild ass that was favored over the domestic donkeys when it came to certain activities.

Now, what is interesting to note is how the donkey actually became domesticated. It is possible that these animals replaced the ox as the chief pack animal back in that time. When these animals were domesticated, they made mobility of these people easier because they did not have to take breaks to chew cud like the other ruminants like the cow or the ox.

Between 2675-2565 BC, wealthy members in the Dynasty IV era in Egypt actually had close to 1000 donkeys that were used as pack animals, as a source of meat or even to assist in agriculture.

By the time the fourth millennium BC had ended, these creatures had made their way down to Southwest Asia. The main breeding area of donkeys had changed to Mesopotamia around 1800 BC. In Damascus, large white assess meant particularly for riding became popular. In Syria, on the other hand, more than three breeds of donkeys were developed. These creatures were considered perfect for women to ride on because of the relaxed gait. The famous Yemen ass or Muscat ass was developed in Arabia.

Donkeys were brought to Europe around the second millennium BC around the same time as viticulture or the making of wine was introduced. This is a theory because donkeys have often been associated with Dionysus, the Syrian god of wine. The Greeks brought these to a lot of their colonies including the ones that are in France, Spain and Italy. It was the Romans who actually spread them around the Empire.

Donkeys were brought to America for the first time during the Second Voyage of Christopher Columbus. They were taken to Hispaniola in about 1495 AD.

The first time donkeys were introduced to South America was when they were taken to Mexico by the first Bishop of the land, Juan de Zumarraga. This was on 6th December 1528.

It is possible that the donkeys were first brought to the United States in April 1598 by a man named Juan de Onate. From then on, their importance in mines and other areas of labor became known. In fact, they were heavily documented around 1679 in the Arizonian areas.

They became the first preference as a beast of burden by the time the Gold Rush occurred in the 19th Century. At least in the western region of the

United States, the donkey had become completely irreplaceable. Several donkeys were later abandoned or had escaped when the mining boom ended. That gave birth to a wild or feral population that is still seen today.

2. Donkeys at work

It is not news that donkeys have been of great economic importance to people for time immemorial. For over 5000 years, they have played the part of a working animal in human civilization. In this section, we will discuss the economic and other uses of the donkey.

a. Economic uses

There are more than 40 million donkeys in the world today. Of these, 96% are in rural areas and under developed countries. Here, the role of these donkeys is primarily to work as a pack animal or to transport agriculture and supplies in draught-ridden areas.

It is believed that after human beings, donkeys are the next cheapest source of agricultural power. You can ride a donkey, raise water, use them for milling and threshing or other related work. Donkeys are often associated with people who live at subsistence levels or lower than that. In many cultures it is a taboo for women to work with oxen in the fields. However, working with donkeys is not really an issue. That makes the donkey a more favorable choice for just about anyone to use on a farm.

In countries that are more developed, donkeys are no longer the beasts of burden. Instead they serve the role of guarding sheep or siring miles. It is also believed that when donkeys are kept amidst horses, they have a calming effect even on the nervous horses. It has been observed in stables that have mares with calves that the young ones often turn to the donkey when they are looking for support after being weaned from their mother.

In a very small part of the world, donkeys are actually raised as a source of meat. In Italy and areas of Europe, especially, equine meat is quite popular. Here, the meat of the donkey is the main ingredient in several local dishes. About 100 tons of meat is generated by slaughtering close to 1000 donkeys. This makes them an economical source of meat as well.

In Italy, donkey milk is considered to be very good for your health and is actually quite expensive. It costs about 15 euros a liter. This milk is not just used in foods but is also an important ingredient in soaps and cosmetics. This market for the meat and milk of the donkey is expanding fast. Several years ago, the skin of a donkey served the purpose of parchment paper!

In China, donkey meat is considered a delicacy. There are several restaurants that specialize in cooking and serving the meat of donkeys! It might make you cringe, but donkey genitalia are served as expensive delicacies. The gelatin produced by stewing soaked donkey hide is used in traditional remedies of Chinese medicine.

b. Donkeys in warfare

For an animal that is considered so dull and stupid, the donkey was actually given a very important role to play in the First World War. A British Stretcher bearer used the donkey to rescue soldiers from the Australian and New Zealand Army Corps during the battle of Gallipoli. A similar role was given to the donkey by Richard Alexander Henderson from the New Zealand Medical Corps.

Additionally, it was noted by a British author, Matthew Fort that donkeys also helped the Italian Army during this period. Every Mountain Fusilier was given an individual donkey to carry their gear. There was another purpose for having a donkey in the army: if the troops had to face any adverse conditions, the meat of the donkey could be consumed for survival.

In war-ridden regions like Afghanistan, donkeys are used even today to carry explosives and other ammunition.

What caught the attention of human beings over the several centuries of association with the donkey is the fact that this creature is extremely hardy. In addition to that, they are inexpensive and extremely under-demanding. These creatures were among the easiest to herd and could be easily managed irrespective of the gender and irrespective of whether it was a group or an individual handling them.

These characteristics made the donkey an important part of human civilization. They have actually motorized several tribes and groups with great ease.

3. Types of donkeys

Since the time the stereotypes referring to donkeys have been erased, these creatures have garnered a lot more interest across the globe and have been bred for different purposes. Today, donkeys are bred to be good riding animals, companions for livestock, novelty cart pulling animals and also guardians of flocks. This interest in donkeys has given birth to several breeds that are rather interesting. It is believed that the age we live in is the renaissance for donkeys. So, if you are looking at bringing one home as a pet, here are the options that you can choose from:

- **The standard donkey:** These are the creatures that we normally picture when we think of donkeys. They measure between 36 to 48 inches at the shoulder. These animals are equipped to do just about anything. From being a pack animal to guarding flocks to even babysitting the younger stock, they can do it all. These donkeys are not tall enough for you to ride comfortably. However, they are certainly the most versatile of all the donkey breeds that you will come across.

- **Mammoth donkey:** Also known as the American Mammoth, this is the largest species of donkey that you will see. They measure between 54 (females) to 56 (males) inches at the shoulder. These donkeys were initially bred in order to provide mates for horses. This resulted in the birth of the mule. These tall donkeys were a pleasure to ride as they had the perfect gait. They were able to sustain long rides that let the rider actually enjoy the scenery and the journey. In addition to that, these creatures were not as skittish as horses. This meant that they would not bolt off while you were still on a trail, unlike horses.

- **Miniature:** These donkeys are the best option if you are looking for a pet. They are also called the miniature Mediterranean donkey. They are originally from Italy. These cute creatures have often been raised as great companions for horses. Now, they do not grow larger than 36 inches at the shoulder even after attaining complete maturity. The miniature donkey is very laid back and peaceful. They have been raised to be friendly, lovable and extremely social. They are the most popular choice as pets as they are extremely adorable in their appearance and also very approachable in their demeanor.

- **Poitou:** The French Poitou is one of the newest breeds of donkeys. It is found very rarely in the United States and is known for distinguishing characteristics like its long coat. This coat is also known as the cadenette. During the warmer months, this undercoat molts. Maintenance is one issue with this breed of donkey. It is possible that the undercoat and the outer coat get tangled when you do not take good care of it. Now, if you are looking particularly for a Poitou, you may find it harder to obtain one as they are very rare world over. However, you can connect with Donkey clubs like the American Donkey and Mule Society to look for specific breeds.

- **Spotted Ass:** Usually a donkey is brown or gray in color. In some cases, there may be interbreeding between these two varieties, giving birth to the spotted ass. These animals that are mottled beautifully come in several sizes and are known for being rare and exotic. They actually look quite flashy and because they are novel in their appearance, people prefer them as pets. These animals are rare, no doubt. However, the increased interest in the breed has led to an increase in numbers over the years. The issue with this breed is that even if you use a spotted male and female donkey, there is no guarantee that the offspring is spotted as well.

- **Burro:** In the Spanish-speaking world, the term burro is used to refer to both domesticated and wild donkeys. In the rest of the world, however, this word is reserved for donkeys that are free range and wild, mostly in the west. Every year, several such burros are rounded up by the Bureau of Land Management and put up for adoption. They charge an adoption fee of $125 and people actually invest in them to get a "part of the Wild West". These animals are popularly adopted as companions for livestock. They are extremely hardy and are usually the size of a regular donkey. The only thing you need to be aware of with this type is that they are wild and will need extensive training in order to fit in.

- **The mule:** Although it is not a type of breed of donkey, the mule does deserve a place in this list, as it is a favorite among donkey lovers. It is half a donkey genetically. However, you get the agility of the horse and the disposition of the donkey rolled into one hardy creature. This makes them a prized possession. Mules are like donkeys in a lot of ways. Particularly, they have a very strong sense of self-preservation. However, if you are able to gain their trust, they can be molded to perform just about any function on the farm. This hybrid is also known to love children and is therefore very popular. Now, the mule, which is a mix between a male donkey and a female horse, is popular globally. However, the hinny, which is the product of a female donkey and a male horse, is not so common because of chromosomal issues as well as several issues related to the size.

Once you have decided what kind of donkey you want for your home, you can look for a farm or a breeder that specializes in one. No matter what breed you decide to bring home, what you need to remember is that the care that they require is identical. So, the preparations that you have to make to bring any one of them home remains the same.

4. Donkey terms you should know

When you are learning about donkeys, there are a few words that you will have to remember with reference to these creatures. You will have to learn the different words associated with the hybrids and gender of the donkey. That way when you are actually going out to purchase a donkey to bring home as a pet, you will get the right one.

- **Ass:** This is the term used to refer to the animal that belongs to the genus Equus Asinus. The hoarseness of the bray or the voice of this species depends upon a certain cavity that is located just at the bottom of the larynx. Collectively, they are referred to as a pack of asses.

- **Donkey:** This is a term in the English language that is believed to have originated from the Flemish word donnekijn. As per most authorities, this word is derived from the grey brown or the dun color of the animal. The suffix "key" is added to connote that it is small in size. So if you translate the word donkey it means "little dun animal". A group of donkeys is referred to as a herd of donkeys.

- **Moke:** This is a common term used to refer to a donkey in several parts of Great Britain. The term was first used by the Romano people who lived in this region. This term is derived from a Romano or Welsh word, mokhio, which means ass.

- **Jenny or Jennet:** This is the term used for a female donkey.

- **Jack:** This is the term used for a stallion donkey or a male donkey.

- **Geldling:** A gelded or a spayed donkey stallion is referred to with this term.

- **Hinny or Mule:** As discussed before, these terms are used to refer to a hybrid between a donkey and a horse. In 99.9% of these hybrids, the specimen is sterile. When they are in a group, they are referred to as a barren of hinnies or mules.

- **Molly:** When a male donkey and a female horse produce a female mule, it is called a Molly.

- **John:** When a male donkey and a female horse produce a male mule, it is referred to as a John.

- **Foal:** A baby donkey or a baby mule is referred to as a foal.

These terms will make it easier for you to communicate with a breeder or someone at a farm when you decide to bring home a pet donkey.

5. Donkey behaviour

Any difference in behavior of a certain species is the result of the initial stages of evolution. Now, most people think that equine behavior is similar. However, donkeys and horses are very different because of the way that they evolved.

Now, as for horses, they have always grown and evolved as herd animals. There are two possibilities when it comes to donkeys. If the environment is nutritionally rich, then they stay together as herds. The jacks are most territorial in these herds.

On the other hand, if vegetation is limited and the availability of water is restricted, the mares will separate from the herd and will either live alone or with their offspring from the previous breeding season. Then, in the breeding season, the males tend to dominate a certain area in order to find a mate. This is the basic cause for a very marked difference between donkey and horse behavior. Not understanding these behaviors often leads to a lot of issues with the behavior of donkeys that have been domesticated. The difference in the social structure is responsible for all the changes in the behavior between horses and donkeys.

In the case of horses, they had to simply outrun a member in the herd in order to survive. But, in the case of donkeys, the numbers never mattered and they usually remained solitary. So, they are genetically predisposed to being fighting animals. In fact, their fight mechanism is so powerful that they make the best guard animals for herds of goats and sheep. They are particularly effective against canine family predators.

This tendency to be dominating has led to very peculiar behavior during domestication. They actually become territorial over the pasture that they are raised in. When not trained properly, they will become a hazard to small pets and livestock. This behavior is not common in all donkeys, however. Some of them are happy to live with the smaller domestic animals. This behavior is predominant in young male donkeys when the environment does not provide ample mental stimulation. In rare cases, this behavior is seen in the older male and female donkeys as well.

Donkeys are known to be very stoic. This means that they will not exhibit pain or fear as easily as horses. Now, this becomes a challenge for the owner of the donkey. You see, even in the case of the most extreme illness, the only thing you will see in a donkey is very minor behavioral changes.

Even when expressing fear, donkeys are quite reserved. You will never see a donkey panic easily. This is why it is harder to deal with donkeys in comparison to horses as opposed to popular belief. When a horse is scared, it is very easy to tell. But the donkey will merely rise up in height and you may see that his/her eyes widen a little. This is commonly mistaken to be excitement or increased interest in an activity or in the immediate environment.

The image that has been projected about the donkey is one of the main reasons for the misunderstanding of the animal. They are represented as the beach donkey that is placid or the Christmas animal that is rather angelic. As a result of this, you will see that most people who set out to buy a donkey don't even consider its wild ancestors for a minute. This makes one forget about the flight or fight instinct of the creature. They can be just as challenging as the horse to handle. On the positive side, however, the reduced state of panic in a donkey ensures that injuries to the owner or to the animal itself are not common.

Aggression is normally seen in male donkeys when they become territorial. These episodes can be so bad that they actually draw one another's blood. There are certain horsemanship methods that you can apply with a horse quite easily. This, however, is not the case with donkeys that are more stoic. This makes it harder to force them to do what you want or to get them to perform certain tasks. This is where their reputation of being stubborn comes from. However, when one understands the science of a donkey's behavior, training is easier.

Donkeys respond a lot better to positive reinforcement. With an experienced trainer, clicker training can also be very useful in the case of donkeys. If you have a donkey with a certain phobia, methods like counter-conditioning work really well.

When it comes to training or conditioning a donkey, it is very important to take small steps and then shape the behavior of the donkey. This is true for all animals, in fact. You need to give your pet time to think and understand the behavior that you expect from them. When the problem solving ability kicks in, you will have a well-trained animal.

Now, there is one more aspect of the donkey's behavior that has made them obtain the tag of being stubborn. People often feel like they have to apply a lot of force to get the donkey to walk with them or to even get them to perform routine tasks. The primary cause for this is that the donkey has a very good walking pace. So, instead of getting the donkey to walk at our pace, matching their pace until they are trained can work wonders.

It is important to understand that these creatures also need a lot of stimulation in order to behave well. Donkeys are genetically predisposed to travelling long distances to look for food. However, this is not a requirement when they are domesticated. This leads to a lot of boredom and even over eating, which will lead to several behavioral problems. We will talk about behavioral issues in donkeys in the following chapter to help you understand how you can correct them.

The one thing you should always remember is that any behavior that you see in a donkey is justifiable. Donkeys do not show any reaction without reason. If your donkey is depicting a certain behavior then it definitely is benefiting the donkey. This trait of looking after one's benefits is called self-preserving. This is very high in the case of a donkey. When you remove the benefit, the behavior also stops eventually.

The most important thing to do as a donkey owner is to free yourself from any stereotyping or assumptions about the behavior of the donkey. Look at every donkey as an individual and when you treat them that way you will be able to get them to fit into your life in every possible way.

Chapter 2: Bringing the Donkeys Home

Now that you know what to expect from a donkey, you can bring one home provided you have the space. However, just space is not the only criterion for bringing home a donkey. There are several things that you must consider before you decide to bring home a donkey.

1. Before you bring the donkey home

The responsibility of bringing a donkey home is bigger than you can imagine. There are a few things that you need to make sure that you take care of when you decide to have a pet donkey:

- You need to make sure the environment is suitable.
- You need to provide the donkey with a good diet.
- You need to ensure that he has good company.
- You need to make sure that your donkey is protected from suffering from any kind of disease or injury.

a. Legal considerations

Being a committed donkey owner is not just about morals and ethics. In fact, you can get into legal trouble if you do not ensure the welfare of your donkey or any other equine such as a horse. The above-mentioned points are codes of the Animal Welfare act and any breach in the code is an offence. Even when you are away from your pet, you are responsible under this act.

The Animal Welfare Act states that the duty of care rests in the hands of the keepers and the owners of horses and donkeys irrespective of whether you are caring for the animal temporarily or permanently. So whether you actually own the donkey or are just in charge of it, the rules apply. The only thing is that the owner has the ongoing responsibility of the donkey even if he/she has hired someone else to be "in charge".

Now, if you are looking at buying your child a pet in order to help them learn about the responsibility of owning a pet, then you are responsible if the child is 16 years of age or younger.

If you are going to be away from your pet, you need to make sure that the person you leave him/her with is competent enough to handle any emergency. They should also have the authority to take decisions for your pet in your absence.

The responsibility of owning a donkey includes a detailed understanding of the specific health requirements of the animal as well as the welfare of the animal. You need to have the necessary skills to take care of the donkey. You will also have to understand the Code of Practice as per your area of residence. If you are unsure, make sure that you have the right sources to seek advice from when required.

b. Other considerations

While it is great fun to own a donkey and is actually quite rewarding, you need to be aware of the fact that it is a big responsibility. There are a few considerations that you should keep in mind when you do decide to bring a donkey home:

- **If you are taking care of the animal on a short term basis:** Even if the animal has been taken into your care for fostering or as a loan from a farm or a certain activity, the responsibility is the same as owning a horse.

- **It is not financially easy to own a donkey:** If you think that a stack of hay is good enough for your donkey, you are wrong. You need to take care of several things such as the housing area of the donkey, the kind of food that he/she needs, any health issues and specifications and lots more. You will have to make a budget based on your own needs and requirements to see if you can fit a donkey into it. The costs you must include are:
  - The bedding
  - Food
  - The pasture and stable
  - Worming
  - Veterinary fees
  - Insurance

- **What kind of donkey works best for you:** This is also very important to understand. Do you want a miniature or a large donkey? The other factors to consider are gender, breed, age and the purpose of getting the donkey home. It is a good idea to see all the options available with breeders to choose one that is most appropriate for your requirements. You should also be compatible with the breed and the temperament. Before you make any decision about your donkey, it is good to consult an equine expert who can give you all the information that you need with respect to purchasing a healthy donkey.

- **Do you have any experience:** Having proper knowledge with respect to caring for the donkey is a must. As mentioned before, you will not get a lot of practical advice, as donkey owners are rare. So, you will need to gain some experience with this animal by visiting farms, stables or even by doing voluntary work with shelters.

- **Have a contingency plan:** This is very important in case of an emergency. You should have several options for transporting your pet in the case of an emergency. Other considerations include transport, stabling and emergency veterinary care. If there is a need to quarantine your donkey in the future, you will need a separate space. You also need to have alternative arrangements to take care of your donkey if you are travelling or if the keeper is unavailable for some reason. When there is any change in the circumstance of the owner, the donkey or even the keeper, you will have to reconsider all the contingency options.

When you have understood the Code of Practice clearly with respect to the welfare of your donkey, you can be sure if you will be comfortable taking care of the donkey. Once you have this in place, you have the task of actually choosing a donkey that will work well for you. Make sure you choose a healthy donkey to avoid unwanted inconvenience and, not to mention, exuberant costs to care for him/her.

2. Buying a donkey
You have the option of buying a donkey from a ranch, a farm or from a shelter. The other option is to adopt a donkey from a shelter. With the latter, the donkey is usually very lonely or abused. That will lead to behavioral issues that can only be handled if the individual has ample experience with equines.

As you know, there are different breeds of donkeys and each one has a specialty of its own. So, whether you want a miniature donkey to be your companion or whether you are looking for a guard donkey, you can choose the donkey based on your requirements. However, the more important factors when it comes to deciding which donkey to bring home are the health of the donkey and the temperament. Here are a few considerations that you need to make when you are planning to bring a donkey home:

a. What to look for
If you are bringing a donkey home, you need to take a look at the company that the donkey has been in. Ideally, you must only buy donkeys in pairs. A lonely donkey will develop several behavior issues. If you are buying a foal, you need to make sure that he/she has been with his mother at least

until the age of one. There are several ways you can judge the age of the donkey. This will be discussed in the following sections.

If you are a farmer who is purchasing a donkey, then buying a castrated male will not work for you. However, if you have a clear purpose for buying the donkey, this may not be an issue.

Most often, a donkey is bought as a working animal, although they are intended to be kept as pets. They may have to perform more than one task, which means that they need to begin training at an early age. That is when you can alter the characteristics of the animal as you like. Of course, every donkey that you bring home must be trained up to some level to make sure that they can coexist with you in your home.

It is best that you visit the donkey that you have chosen to adopt a couple of times before you actually bring him/her home. That will help you observe the way the donkey functions and work. You can decide if he/she is a good fit for your home based on that.

If you are buying an older donkey, ask for the name. Some people who do not treat the donkey like a pet or with enough care will not even name it. That is a good way to know if you are getting a donkey that has been in good hands. In addition to that, knowing the donkey's name will help you build a good relationship with the animal after you bring it home.

In many parts of the world, showing and judging donkeys is highly encouraged to ensure that they are taken good care of. With prizes being awarded to the owners, there is more hope that these animals are not just treated like beasts of burden.

b. Looking for desirable physical traits
When you buy a donkey, you should watch for the following traits to ensure that you have an animal that is healthy. These traits are also used to judge a donkey during shows:

- Large size
- The size of the leg should be equal to the length of the body
- The forelimbs must appear straight from all angles
- The hind legs must look straight when seen from the back
- The back should be parallel to the ground
- The neck should be straight
- The ears should be unbroken
- The hoofs must be properly angled
- The underside of the hoof should be concave

- The teeth should meet squarely and should be uniform and regular in shape
- The body must not have any scars
- The coat should be shiny
- The mane must be thick
- The underside of the hoof should be clean
- The hoofs should be shiny and smooth
- The ribs must not be visible
- The hip bones should be well covered
- The belly must be flat
- The ears must be alert
- The eyes should be alert
- The eyes must be dry
- The teeth should be clean and sound

The next thing to check for is the movement of the donkey:
- The strides must be long
- It should not have any up and down movement in the back
- It should be able to walk fast

The final and most important thing to watch is the temperament of the donkey:
- It should be calm even when there are strangers around
- It should be calm when other donkeys are present
- It should be able to stay comfortably around animals belonging to other species
- It must obey the signs of the handler immediately
- It should stand still when the harness is being put on

If you are looking for a donkey to work on your farm, here are the things you should observe:
- The donkey should be able to plough and make a 50m long straight furrow in a minute
- It should be able to complete a zigzag obstacle course in 1 minute with a loaded cart
- It should be able to pull a cart up a slope without panting too much
- It should be able to bring a fully loaded cart down the slope without slipping
- It should be able to back a fully loaded cart for at least 10m in one straight line
- It should be able to drag a 5m long pole on flat land easily

A perfect donkey is not a possibility. You will find a mixture of desirable traits in each donkey that will help you choose. The only compromise that you should not make is the health of the donkey.

c. Choosing a donkey based on purpose
The role that the donkey will play in your home or in the farm will be a deciding factor when it comes to choosing the donkey. Here are a few tips that should be able to help you make that decision:

Donkeys that are best suited for carrying loads

When you want the donkey to primarily carry loads, the back and legs must be extremely strong. That way, the donkey will be able to carry the load as well as not stumble while doing so. The whole weight, as you know, must be moved around with its tiny feet. So, if you want a donkey that can carry loads, look for:

- Large overall size
- Straight legs
- Well angled feet
- Good eyesight
- Straight back
- Large hooves

The temperament is also important. If the donkey has the habit of fleeing at the sight of a threat, it will be a hassle. It should also obey promptly in order to respond better to any danger such as wild animals. The donkey should be nimble as well.

Donkeys that are best suited for riding
You can consider a person a load that the donkey will carry. In that sense, you want the same physical characteristics. However, in this case the desirable characteristics are very important. The donkey must never stumble. In addition to that, he/she should be prompt in obedience and should be alert and agile.

Donkeys that are best suited for farms
If the donkey is being chosen to carry out agricultural work, you will probably need it to pull carts and ploughs. In that case, you need a donkey with very strong shoulders and chest muscles. In addition to that, the legs should be very strong to give the animal the necessary power. So a donkey that is meant for agricultural work should have these characteristics:
- The chest should be wide and deep

- It should be large in size
- The back must be straight
- The legs must be straight and well-muscled

Behavior is also an important factor. He/she should have a lot of endurance to pull for long periods of time. The breathing ability should be good. He/she should also be patient and willing. A good thing to check would be how long the donkey is able to stand in one place.

d. Gender roles of donkeys

The reproductive hormones make a big difference in the behavior of a donkey. The only way to say that a donkey is perfect for your home is when they have the desirable characteristics that will not change except for the effects of disease and old age. Here are the traits you can expect from different genders of donkeys:

Females or Jennies: When a female is in heat, the only thing that she will be after is a male donkey that she desires. She will leave all her work and friends for this. If you do not have a male on the pasture, she can become disobedient until you have her impregnated. When it comes to the females that are feeding, you do not have to worry about pregnancies, but they will still come into heat at times.

You can never tell if a donkey is pregnant. However, when the pregnancy is towards the end, she becomes extremely docile. Of course, during this stage, you cannot use her for any work, as it is hazardous to the fetus. After she has given birth to a foal, she will not be able to work for various weeks, as she will have to feed and nurture the little one.

Males or Jacks: A male that is fully intact is usually very hard to control. They will become even more difficult to manage if there is a female in heat around them. They will also pursue a mate without paying attention to their work and their companions. They also become very dominant over other males who are fully sexed. These fights can be very damaging. These donkeys even tend to attack young donkeys that are still being fed by the mother. They tend to resent the presence of younger donkeys.

Castrated males: Without any doubt, these are the best donkeys to have. Their behavior becomes a lot calmer and the donkey tends to "slow down". They also develop a good amount of fat, which makes them less prone to harness sores. A male that is castrated also uses less energy to do the same amount of work. They are less excitable because of their lack of sexual urges. However, they are extremely alert and responsive. If you are thinking of bringing home a pet, a castrated male is the best option. Of course, breeding is not an option with a castrated donkey.

How to determine the gender of a donkey

In the case of the younger donkeys or foals, identifying the gender is very difficult. You will not be able to see the reproductive organs easily. Placing your hand on the belly and sliding it across will be able to help you determine the gender. However, this can be misleading if the umbilical cord is still present. To determine the gender, lifting the tail is the best way to identify if it is a female. However, this can be dangerous and you should only attempt to check this when the tail is voluntarily lifted to swat flies, defecate or urinate.

In the case of the males, you will often find it challenging to determine the sex because the penis is retracted. The penis also has a sheath with a protrusion that resembles a nipple. This will often be confused for an udder, making one determine the gender incorrectly. In this section you will learn about determining the gender of the donkey correctly:

Female: The female has an udder with two teats that is usually hidden between the back legs. The fluffy coat makes it hard to see this when the donkey is younger. Of course, you can feel this organ when you put your hand on the belly. Another way to check if the donkey is a female is when the tail is lifted. If you can see a two stage slit just below the anus, it is a female donkey.

Male: The penis sheath of the male is held close to the body and in the exact place as the udders in the female donkeys. That is very hard to see when the donkey is young. You also have the nipple-like protrusions, which make it very hard for a novice to determine the gender. The advantage is that the penis of the animal is extended when they are urinating. The penis also becomes more visible when the male grows older. The scrotum will drop when the donkey is about one and a half years or two years old.

Castrated male: If the donkey is over two years in age but the scrotum is still not seen, then there are chances that it is a castrated male.

If you are unable to determine the gender of the donkey, it is best that you have a vet help you check.

e. Adopting a donkey

Donkeys are put up for adoption for various reasons. Sometimes they are rescued from poor living conditions and abusive homes. Other times the owners give the donkey up because they are unable to care for it. Now, if you are looking for adoption, it will mean two things in the case of large animals like the donkey:

- **You pay for their care:** You can visit a shelter near your home or even look up several online options to pay for a donkey to help the facility care for the donkey. This is the best option if you are a first timer in the world of donkeys. You can adopt a donkey from a shelter nearby and then visit him or her often. Then, if you are certain that they fit into your home and the environment at your pasture, you can bring them home.

- **You choose a donkey you want to bring home:** This is an option only for the experienced donkey owners. You need to make sure that you are fully aware of the behavioral issues that can develop in a lonely and abandoned donkey. Unless you can commit to training and working on the issues that the donkey might have, adopting from a shelter is not the best idea.

3. Preparing for a donkey

The most important thing that you need to do is prepare your space for the donkey's arrival. The space that you provide will determine the health and mental stability of your beloved pet. You will have to make a shelter for your donkey. We will learn in detail about the housing options in the following chapters. The donkey needs to be protected from winds, flies and even the scorching summer sun. You must also have a spare shelter if you already have equines in your home in case of any emergency quarantining requirements.

a. Preparing the pasture

The area of the pasture is the first thing that you must consider. Each donkey will require between 0.4 hectares per individual. This requirement depends on the conditions of the ground, the season, the type of grass on the pasture and the pasture management efforts from your end. Now, if you have a smaller area, it is ok as long as your donkey is housed in the shelter principally and uses the grazing areas occasionally.

You will need to employ a good pasture management program to ensure that the donkeys do not over graze and to also ensure that you are able to control worms, provide good drainage and also control weed growth. Good pasture management includes activities like the removal of the droppings, regularly rotating the grazing area and preventing the donkey from entering any wet, muddy area.

b. Keeping the pasture safe

There are several types of plants that are toxic to donkeys and horses. These should be removed from the area to keep the animal safe. Ragwort, for instance, is very toxic. Any ingestion can lead to severe damage in the liver. It is a good idea to read pasture guides about the removal and control of ragwort weed. These plants, when merely cut, remain toxic to donkeys. You will have to remove them completely and also dispose of them correctly.

You must also remember that every part of this weed is poisonous for humans as well. So, gloves must be worn when you are pulling or cutting the weed.

Even pulling is not enough in the case of flowering ragwort plants. You can consult a professional to help you effectively remove the weed. One of the best options is incineration or controlled burning. There are other plants such as laburnum and yew that are toxic to donkeys. You must make sure that they do not have access to these plants in any form.

Grass cuttings are also not advisable for donkeys and they should be kept away from garden waste of any kind.

Lastly, you need to remove any object that can cause injuries to your donkey. Any sharp projections or unstable objects that may fall or injure the animal should be removed immediately. Leveling the ground on a regular basis also prevents a lot of injuries in the case of donkeys walking around free range. This prevents stumbling and any bone or muscle injury to the animal.

4. Donkeys and other pets

If you have a pet dog or cat at home and want your donkey to mix with them, it may not be the best idea. Now, instinctively, donkeys are guard animals that are meant to ward off canine predators and other predators. So, in all probability, your donkey will consider your pet a threat to its well being or the well being of its companions.

The donkey is a docile creature, no doubt. But, at the same time, you must never underestimate the power of a donkey. All it really takes is one kick for your dog to be severely injured. In some cases, the kick can also be a threat to your dog's life. Now, that said, you do not have to completely drop the idea of bringing a donkey home if you have a pet dog or cat. Here are some options that you can try:

- Keep them in separate areas even on the pasture. You can have a portable fence that the donkeys can stay in when your dogs are out. This is a very important measure if you see any aggression from the dogs towards the donkey or vice versa. In most cases, a well-trained dog will be easy to handle even without the fence as long as you are supervising the interactions.

The fence is a good option for introductions. You can keep the animals separated by a portable fence and watch their body language. Any discomfort or unnecessary excitement will become obvious to you. When you see the dog and the donkey oblivious to each other's presence, you can safely let them out of the fence but only when they are under supervision.

- Work on training your pets. Just like dogs, donkeys can also be trained for obedience commands like recall. This is very important when you have mixed animal species on your pasture. Similarly, you have to train the dog well, too. If your dog is not fully trained or is still a puppy, you must always keep him/her away from the donkey unless you are confident that they are completely under your control.

If you are looking for guard animals on a farm for your livestock, then having donkeys and dogs on the farm is a great idea. Donkeys are able to keep most predators away. However, in the case of some predators like bob cats or jungle cats, dogs are able to handle them a lot better.

The best precaution you can take is to select a donkey with a calm temperament when you have other pets at home. You must always be aware of the fact that there is a small amount of risk when you are placing these animals in one area. So, in case of any accident or untoward incident, you must remember never to blame the donkey or the dog. They react out of their instincts always and never cause any harm or damage intentionally. If you want your pets to be safe, taking complete precaution is your responsibility.

5. Donkeys and kids

The good news for all donkey owners is that donkeys are naturally conditioned to being great around children. In most cases, homes that have kids would prefer a miniature donkey that will be easier to handle and can even make a wonderful ride for the kids every once in a while.

That said, you must never forget that even with a very gentle donkey, you are dealing with an instinctive being. You have to learn and teach your child how to approach the donkey to ensure that they are completely safe. Here are a few tips that will help:

- Never startle the animal. Tell your child never to shout or scream when they are approaching the animal. It is natural for a child to be excited when they see a furry creature and they tend to make loud noises of approval. While you know that the child is excited, the donkey is going to respond to the sound.

- Always approach the animal slowly. Children tend to run towards an animal and embrace them by the muzzle. This is dangerous if the temperament of the donkey is not entirely known to you. It is best that you silently and calmly approach the donkey.

- The best thing to do would be to stand at a distance from the donkey with the child and wait for the donkey to approach you. If it is calm and the ears are flat to the side, then it means that the donkey is relaxed. If you see that the ears drop down and are flipped back, you must never approach the donkey. This is its warning sign to you that it does not like what is going on at that moment. Donkeys can be vicious in fight mode and you must never let a child approach it.

- You need to learn to interact with the animal first. Before you can introduce the child to the donkey without any physical barrier, you should know exactly how to approach a donkey safely. If you have doubts about this, it is a risk to let your child into the donkey's space.

- Let the child accompany you in routine activities like feeding and filling the water troughs. This is the safest way to get the donkey to become aware of the presence of the child and also learn the scents associated with you and your entire family.

The only time that a donkey and a child may have a confrontation is if you fail to educate the child about properly dealing with the donkey. Most human beings, adults included, often fall short when it comes to interacting with other species.

You have to inform your child that verbal communication does not mean anything to the animal. So kind words does not mean that the donkey will be friendly towards you. Use little verbal communication and try to deal with the animal calmly. Teaching your child this skill will make them have safe and enjoyable interactions with the donkey. However, you must never leave a child unsupervised when a donkey is around.

Chapter 3: Caring for a Donkey

If you provide the right care for your donkey, then you can be assured of a great companion. There are several things that you need to do when you are taking ownership of a donkey. We will discuss all of the donkey's requirements in detail in this chapter.

1. Fencing options

There are several fencing options when it comes to donkeys. You will have to choose one that is the safest for your pet based on the surroundings of your pasture and the possible threats to your donkey. Here are the four most popular options:

a. Board fences

These fences are also called rail fences, plank or post fences and are very popular on farms because they look very nice. They are very easily visible to the animal and they are quite safe. These fences have treated wood planks that are screwed on to wooden posts. They may also be made of wooden rails that fit into slots on wooden posts or can be constructed from PVC plastic posts and boards. The biggest advantage with this type of fencing is that they are very economical. When maintained properly, they can easily last for about 25 years.

The wooden planks are most often made from oak that is treated and rough-cut. With rough-cut oak, you have the advantage of a rustic appearance. Oak is also a sturdy material that will remain intact, even if an animal leans on it. The good thing is that donkeys do not like to chew on planks made of oak.

What you need to watch out for is warping of the board when it is freshly cut. In case there are any spots on the plank that have been weakened naturally, it may lead to the fence rotting quickly. Oak rots faster than any other type of wood. With treated pine, you have a good finish and it even takes paint quite well, although not easily. When treated, pine does not rot very easily. It also keeps donkeys away and discourages chewing. You have to keep up the treatment regularly, as it can wear off. Since pine is not too strong, you will have to opt for thicker boards.

b. Vinyl fences

You can use solid PVC plastic to make fences. They are a lot more expensive than wooden planks. This is because they require painting. However, in terms of maintenance, they cost a lot less.

You also have the option of vinyl-dipped fences that consist of wooden planks that are dipped in vinyl. This is not as durable, as the chance of warping is still high. In the southern states, mildew is a problem if you have white fencing.

c. Cattle Panels

Also known as stock panels, these are fabricated mesh fences that are usually made from galvanized steel. The rods are about ¼ inch in width. These fences are about 52 inches in height and have stays that are 8 inches thick.

The close-set, horizontal wires are tighter at the bottom to ensure that the smaller livestock do not escape. This is also extremely useful in keeping small predators out of your pasture. You can trim the panels as required, as they come in rolls that are 16 feet in length. All you need is a heavy bolt cutter.

You also have sheep panels that are about 40 inches high. The wires in this case are set closer to one another. The best type of panels is utility panels, which are extremely tough. They are made using 4-inch spacing and extra heavy-duty 4-6 gauge rods. They are usually 20 feet in length and between 4-6 feet in height.

These panel fences are best to make stout corrals that last long, are economical and maintenance free. You have to be very cautious about the raw ends of the rod in each panel. They can be very sharp and can cause serious damage to your donkey. You need to make sure that you smooth out each sharp end using a rasp to take off the razor sharp edge.

d. Woven wire fences

Also known as a field fence or a wire mesh, a woven wire fence is one of the best options for a large area. They are made with several lines of smooth wire held apart using a stay, which is a vertical wire.

The spacing between these horizontal wires is close at the bottom. Usually, the woven wire meshes are about 6 inches apart and have stays that are 12 inches long.

The biggest disadvantage with these fences is that they can be extremely expensive. However, in terms of security, they are the best. That is why they are great to mark the boundary of your pasture.

Most predators will be kept at bay when you use the wire fencing. They are about four feet in height and are ideal for all equines, especially miniature donkeys. If required, you can also install an electric wire above the fence for additional safety.

You can check the quality of the wire with the help of a few numbers that are printed on it. For example, if your fence reads 10-47-6-9, it means that the fence has 10 horizontal wires that have 6 inch spacing between them. The height is 47 inches and the wire used is a 9-gauge wire.

If you want a high tensile wire, it is more expensive than standard ones. However, it will not rust or sag over time. It is also a lot lighter in weight.

These woven wires come with aluminum or zinc wiring. The coating is classified as Class I, II or III. Class III denotes the thickest coating. The higher the number, the more durable the fencing.

e. Kinds of fencing to avoid

In 1999, a fence safety survey was conducted by the Equine research Center in Guelph, Canada. This test was based on 180 horse owners who also owned donkeys and mules. On the positive side, 73% of these owners revealed that they had no injuries in the past year with their animals. However, with the remaining 27%, it was noted that the injuries were mostly fence related. Some of the injuries were so bad that the animal required veterinary care immediately. Here are some pointers that will help you understand the situations in which injuries are highly likely:

- Barbed wired accounted for almost 63% of the injuries. The woven and high tensile wires were responsible for most serious injuries.

- The safest were the diamond mesh woven wires, which caused about 6% of the injuries reported but none of them were serious.

- The board fences caused injuries mostly in horses, as they ran into the fence or kicked them too hard. None of these injuries involved a donkey, however.

- Injuries were reported with electrical tape, but these were only minor injuries.

- Interestingly, when a new animal was added to an established herd, it led to injuries. When the pastures were overcrowded, there were instances of the animals running in to the fences.

One of the most common options for fencing is the barbed wire. This is considered the ideal stockman's fence. However, the injuries caused have been extremely nasty. If you already have barbed wire around your property, it is a good idea to put another type of fencing that will be placed before the barbed wire. If you can replace the barbed wire with a type of fencing that is donkey friendly, it is the best option available.

If you are choosing electric fencing, then make sure that the voltage is controlled. Should the donkey run into it, he/she should only have a small jolt. Electric fences can be dangerous if you do not maintain them properly. They can be fatal for your animal in most cases.

The safest of all fences are the PVC fences. In the study conducted above, no injuries were reported. So, if you are looking for the most reliable option for your pasture, investing in a good quality PVC fence can be a great idea.

The height of the fence is also an important factor in determining the effectiveness of it. Now, if you have a herd of donkeys, you will have to measure the height up to the withers of the tallest donkey. The fence should be higher than this in order to be effective. This will also keep predators like coyotes at bay.

Lastly, make sure that the visibility of the fence is high. Use thicker wires, brighter colors, etc. so that your animal is able to view it from a distance. That will prevent them from running into it and injuring themselves. Although this is an uncommon occurrence with donkeys, taking precautions is the responsibility of the owner.

2. Shelter requirements

Proper shelters are extremely important for your donkey. When the weather is not suitable or if the animal wants to simply rest, having good housing is a must. There are three things that you must consider when it comes to the shelter of the donkey:

- It should be free from the risk of catching fire
- It should have adequate ventilation and drainage
- There should not be any risk of injury due to poor construction.

When you are planning a housing area for your donkey, here are the things that you must consider:

a. Construction

The construction should ensure that there are no projections on the surface of the stable or the shelter to prevent injury. You must clean all the exposed surfaces and disinfect them to ensure the good health of your herd. If you are using treated wood or any paint on the surface of the construction material, it should not be toxic to donkeys. Wooden material requires preservatives to prevent any chance of rotting or warping.

The flooring should be leveled as much as possible and must not be slippery. Good drainage is necessary to make sure that any stable waste is drained out.

The doors should be at least 4 ft. wide. The height should be such that the donkey is able to look out over the door by placing his head out. Use bolts on the top and bottom to make sure that the door is fastened well when the donkeys are inside. You can even have a top door that can be secured when in the open position. The disadvantage with a top door is that ventilation and sunlight is reduced when it is closed.

The stable should also have good lighting to ensure that the donkey can see. Even the keeper will be able to examine the animal and handle them safely. You can have portable lighting as well. If you do plan to install the lighting inside the shelter, make sure that the bulbs are out of the donkey's reach. The cabling should be secure and of high quality to prevent any chance of fires or short circuits.

The air circulation should be adequate while ensuring that there are no drafts inside the shelter. You can even install safety glass with each window to keep the shelter warm. It is best to keep one window open at all times unless the temperature drops drastically.

If you do not provide enough ventilation, there are chances that your donkey will develop respiratory issues. While airflow should be kept at a maximum, you need to keep a constant check on the dust that is entering the stable.

Ideally, the size of the shelter should be large enough to provide 10ftX12ft for each donkey. This will allow them to rise easily, turn around while inside the stable and also maintain a safe distance from the other donkeys that you may have housed inside the stable. If you have a communal stable that houses a herd, space should be the top priority.

b. Bedding
Keeping your donkeys warm is very important. For this, adequate bedding material is necessary. This not only provides warmth but also protects the animal against any chance of injury. When the donkey lies down on the floor, he/she will be comfortable with good bedding.

The bedding material should be free from mold and too much dust. The material should also be non-toxic to donkeys. The best option is rubber matting, as it is also absorbent by nature. You can even add material like straw, shavings and other material that can absorb any urine. This material should be changed regularly and well managed to ensure complete hygiene and disease prevention.

c. Fire safety

The biggest risk in any stable is fire. You will have to take into consideration all the fire safety recommendations that are made in the "Guide to Fire Safety in Animal Establishments and Stables" laid out by your Local Government.

If you are unsure, you can also seek advice from a Fire Prevention Officer in your locality to understand the statutory requirements. If you have any combustible liquid or material in the barn, it should be removed instantly. You should also make sure that you do not smoke in the stable or in the areas near it.

The fire extinguishers, alarm systems and other equipment should be checked on a regular basis by someone who is qualified. If you have any electrical installations in the barn, they should be periodically inspected and maintained. The fittings and wires should not be accessible to the donkeys.

You must also make sure that it is earthed properly and is kept safe from any rodent. If you need to use extension cables and leads, you should make sure that it does not get entangled in the legs of the animal, leading to serious injuries.

Metal pipe work and any steel that is used in the structure should be earthed well. You can take additional precautions by ensuring that all the installations are protected by an RCD, or a residual current device.

Lastly, in case there is an outbreak of a fire, you must make sure that your animals could be released easily. A fire exit should be installed and an emergency turnout procedure should be planned and communicated to everyone who is working at the stable with the donkeys.

d. Rugs

Not all donkeys need rugs for protection as they are hardy creatures. If they have thick coats, they are additionally equipped to survive harsh winters. However, if the donkey is old, clipped or is not as hardy, you have to keep him/her protected from any draft or low temperature. You can also use these rugs to keep flies at bay. Any turnout rug should be removed in case the weather improves to prevent the stable from getting very warm.

The size of the hood and the rug should be good enough to suit the size of the donkey. You need the right size to ensure that there are no abrasions, hair loss or restricted movements. They should be removed on a regular basis to check the body condition of the donkey. You should also make sure that the donkey does not get too hot because of the rug being on him constantly.

The rugs should be cleaned and repaired regularly. In case of any wetness in the rugs, you should have a spare one that you can use on your donkey. These precautions ensure that the animal stays clear of any illnesses.

e. Tethering
Securing the animal using a chain or any kind of anchorage is called tethering. With this, you are able to confine the donkey in an area that you want him to stay in. Long-term management is not possible with tethering. This makes the animal incapable of exercise and even restricts freedom to a large extent.

You must also consider the possibility of injuries relating to the entangling of the legs. In addition, the animal becomes incapable of escaping predators as well.

Short term tethering, however, can be very useful. If you need to restrict food intake for medical reasons, for instance, tethering becomes important. So, you need to provide some facility where the donkey can be tethered in case of such an emergency.

In case you decide to have your donkey tethered, you need to remember that he/she should be checked on every six hours. That way, you will be aware of any requirement that your donkey may have, such as water or food. You may also have to tether your donkey in order to manage an orthopedic condition. In that case it is mandatory to have controlled exercise sessions to keep your donkey in good shape.

3. Feeding the donkey
The guidelines mentioned in this section are with respect to feeding a healthy adult donkey. Special cases such as a young donkey or a pregnant mare will be discussed in the following chapters.

One of the biggest responsibilities of a donkey owner is to ensure that the pet gets a healthy diet. The genetic history of the donkey shows that these animals originated in the arid regions of Africa. That makes them genetically predisposed to a diet that is high in fiber and very sparse in vegetation.

In the wild, donkeys are browsers. This means that they eat small amounts of food as they wander around. The natural diet of a donkey consists of barks, twigs, thick-stemmed plants, woody herbs, leaves, thistles, blackberries and several other plant varieties. They usually consume food belonging to the non-grass variety, in contrast to popular belief.

When you are feeding a donkey, the first thing you should remember is that the donkey is not similar to the horse in any way. They have an entirely different physiology and digestion. The metabolism of these creatures is drastically different too.

Horses require a high calorie diet that is of very high quality. Giving your donkey this food can actually be hazardous to its health! If you do not provide your donkey with the right kind of food, he/she may become obese and may develop ailments related to the hoof and important body organs such as the liver. A donkey that does not get good food will never live a normal life span, which is about 15-30 years depending upon the quality of life that they get.

In addition to this, you should also understand that the donkey is unlike the cow, sheep or other ruminant and should never be fed like one.

a. Water
Donkeys require a continuous supply of water all day. If you cannot supply fresh water continuously, you should make sure that they have enough clean water to drink. This is imperative to ensure that their welfare needs are taken care of.

Even if you have a pasture that is surrounded by natural sources of water such as streams, rivers or ponds, it is not satisfactory, as the water is usually contaminated. In this case, you have to look for an alternative source of water.

If you have a water source, make sure that it is well maintained. Sources containing a sandy base are not recommended, as they cause a lot of problems for the donkey. Another important issue with natural sources of water is that they get icy cold in winters. During the hot months as well, you have to look for alternative sources of water, as it may get too hot for the donkey to go outside.

The water buckets and troughs have to be fixed at a convenient height. If you have donkeys of different sizes, then the water troughs should be placed properly. In many cases, donkeys that cannot reach the trough will try to paw the water. That way, the chances of the trough getting dislodged increase. This can lead to serious injuries. Keep a check on the water containers to make sure that they are always full.

If your donkeys are stabled, they will need a lot more access to fresh water. You can opt for automatic water supplies, but ensure that you check them regularly to ensure that they are working properly.

Maintenance of the water container is a must. Make sure that it is cleaned regularly. Preventing the build-up of any algae or debris is mandatory. Do not use cleaning substances that may be toxic to the animal.

If your donkey is tethered, you have to refill the water troughs on a regular basis. The water trough should be easy to clean and should be spill proof to ensure that the water does not spill if there is any entangling with the tether.

Donkeys require a lot of water each day. They will need between 25-50 liters depending upon the size of the body. The consumption of water increases in the warmer months. You will also have to take into consideration the changing water requirements. For instance, lactating mares will need a lot more water.

b. Grass
If your donkeys are free range, they will browse around and consume the amount of water that they need. Usually a donkey will need a rotated, mixed pasture that is about ½ an acre in area.

In the native environment, a donkey will consume dry grass and also feed from small bushes. They cannot, however, thrive only on grass. Grass does not have the necessary nutrients and is also too high in moisture content.

You need to make sure that your donkey does not graze or get pasture time when the grass may be more moisture laden. This includes the early mornings and the frosty time of the year. You also need to make sure that they do not consume too much spring grass, as it is too rich for the metabolism of the donkey. If your pasture has a lot of grass, you need to monitor the movement of the donkey.

Consuming too much grass does have a flipside. It can lead to obesity, hoof problems and also colic pain in the donkey. Grass cuttings should never be given to a donkey, as the resulting colic pain can be fatal.

If you are unable to manage the movement of the donkey, you can make use of portable electric fences. That will help you manage the pasture and also restrict the areas that the donkey will move around in. Another way to control the grazing of your donkey is to mow the area before allowing the donkey to graze. This is very important to manage the sugar levels in your donkey's body. In addition to that, you can also control the parasitic worms that may affect the health of the animal.

c. Barley straw and grass hay

The natural dry and high fiber diet of your donkey can be managed with the help of grass hay. This should be a staple in your donkey's diet throughout the year.

Hay should be included in the diet when the pasture is too rich, moist or lush. Donkeys require low protein diets, which can be fulfilled with the help of grass hay in the diet. You must not provide your donkey with any alfalfa hay, as it has about 25% protein content that can actually be too high for your donkey.

Grass hay also helps maintain the dental health of your donkey. Since the hay needs to be chewed well for the animal to consume it, the teeth stay in good condition. That way the necessary nutrients are also released properly. If your donkey is unable to chew the hay properly and digest it, it is the indication of poor dental health that needs to be rectified at the earliest for overall health benefits.

On average, an adult donkey measuring about 230 kilos will need to consume close to 2% of their body weight's equivalent of hay in a day. It depends on the season as well, with the consumption being lowered in the warmer months.

A healthy donkey will eat all day long. So, you need to ensure that you match the appetite of the donkey with food that is low in energy value. That way, you prevent your pet from getting too obese.

Your donkey should have access to a generous quantity of grass hay or barley straw of good quality. You can provide this with the help of a hay net or any other suitable container.

The daily ration of hay or barley straw should be divided into 2 or 3 servings per day. That way they have access to high fiber and low calorie forage all day. Barley straw should be the primary feed. You can also use oat straw if the donkey is old or underweight.

In the case of the younger donkeys that have better teeth, you can use wheat stray that is more fibrous but much lower in the energy value.

d. Salt and mineral blocks
Donkeys need a lot of trace minerals and salts. This can be provided with mineral blocks that are specially designed for the equines. You can place the block in a special container that is designed for it. You can also place it near the water trough. Now, it is important that you do not give your donkey salt blocks that are made for cattle. These are rich in urea that is very unhealthy for a donkey.

e. Treats
Every pet owner wants to spoil his or her pet with a lot of treats and goodies. You can certainly do the same with your donkey. However, the treats that you give your donkey should not be too high in calories and carbs. This leads to digestive issues as well as hoof diseases.

You must avoid lawn clippings and breads that have very high levels of starches and carbohydrates that are unhealthy. You must also limit the amount of treats that you give your donkey.

If your donkey is constantly expecting treats, he will become very agitated and may develop issues like biting if they do not like the treat that they are receiving. One of the best treats to give your donkey is carrots. Cut them lengthwise and offer them to ensure that your donkey does not choke on them.

The eating habits of your donkey must be monitored carefully. These animals will not show any signs of pain or illness. However, they will give you warning signs in the form of a noticeable change in appetite. If you notice any sudden change, make sure that you consult your vet at the earliest.

f. Healthy feeding tips
- Make sure that the food that you give your donkey is good quality. It should be free from any debris, soil or poisonous plants. The food must be visibly free from any dust or mold.

- It is a good idea to feed the donkey at floor level. That keeps their respiratory system in good condition. However, the ground that you feed them on should be very clean.

- The food that you give your donkey should be stored in containers that are vermin proof. That way, it will not spoil easily. You can also ensure that the feeding quality is maintained.

- The feeding container that you use should be kept very clean to prevent any infestation with rodents or vermin. Any remaining food should be cleaned out every day. Each feed should be prepared freshly and should be mixed well.

- In case you are feeding a group of donkeys at once, you must give each donkey an individual feeder. The distance between each feeder should be equivalent to two donkeys' length. That way, you will prevent any risk of food-related competition, which can cause fights among your donkeys.

On a regular basis, make sure that you are monitoring the weight of your donkeys. An increase in weight is an indication of impending obesity that can lead to a lot of metabolic issues in the donkey. If you are making any change in your diet in terms of the volume or the type of food you are providing, do it gradually. If the changes are too sudden, it will lead to colic pain and diarrhea in your donkey.

If you are a first time donkey owner, you should make sure that you consult your vet to understand the correct way to feed your donkey. An equine vet or nutritionist will be able to assess the requirements of your donkey and suggest a diet according to the age and weight.

4. Grooming a donkey

It is important to groom a donkey in order to ensure that the coat stays smooth and shiny. If you plan to enter your donkey into shows, grooming is particularly important. Donkeys will grow a lot of wooly fur during the winter, which needs to be trimmed and maintained in order to keep him/her looking clean and healthy.

a. Trimming the donkey

Now, the mane, the ears, the tail and the under jaw will have a lot of hair that will make the donkey look shabby. You will have to trim this hair to give it a smooth appearance.

You can use scissors to trim the excess hair. You need to make sure that you have scissors with rounded ends to give the donkey a good trim. You can also use dog clippers and razor blades to cut the excess hair. Here are some trimming tips that you need to keep in mind:

- **The jawline:** The long hair from the chin up to the jaw should be trimmed gently. This needs to be done to prevent your donkey from looking like the head just extends into the neck without a proper demarcation. While doing this, remember to get a smooth outline.

- **The mane:** You will need to separate any brown or grey hair that is growing from the neck from the darker strands of hair. You will start trimming near the withers and first cut the pale colored hair. The mane must be cut on either side while ensuring that you do not cut too close to the skin. After you have evenly shortened the hair on both sides, you can cut the rest of the mane to the size that you desire. Hold the hair that you want to cut off between the index finger and the second finger just as a barber would. You can trim the area just behind the ears to make the saddle fit properly.

- **Ears:** It can be a task to cut the hair on the ears, as donkeys hate when their ears are touched. You need to be very patient with this. Start by stroking the ear from the base to the tip. When the donkey is relaxed, you can cup the edges of the ear to move the hair forward. Cut the tips of the hair to level with the edge. You can then trim any hair around the edges.

- **Tail:** The first thing that you need to do is detangle the hair on the tail. This can be done by just running your finger through the hair of the tail. You can then use a currycomb to smoothen it out even more. Trim the hair just below the hocks by about 4 inches. Place your hand under the tail, lift it and then cut at an angle. The top section should be trimmed so that the stubby short hair is removed right to the root of the tail.

- **Hooves:** You will not see any feathers around the hooves in most donkeys. However, if you trim any long hair that may be growing over the face of the hoof, you will get it looking a lot cleaner. The lower legs can be left without trimming if you are not too skilled. This hair growth will fall out on its own after winter is over.

- **Tummy hair:** The tummy hair, too, will fall out eventually. If you groom the donkey every day and brush him, especially, this hair will not be a problem. Avoid trimming it using scissors, as you will leave scissor marks everywhere. In the case of the younger donkeys, leaving the tummy hair is a good idea, as it will give the appearance of great depth in the body that is actually not present.

Trimming the donkey on a regular basis will also help you keep a check on lice, which is a common issue with equines.

b. Bathing a donkey

Lice are extremely common in donkeys, as mentioned above. Giving your donkey an anti-lice bath can prevent the occurrence of these parasites. Along with clipping, bathing is a good option to keep your donkey well groomed. It is good to bathe your donkey after you have clipped off any excess fur. That way, the disinfecting shampoo will reach the skin of the donkey.

Adult lice actually drown when you bathe the donkey. The lice can pose a threat, which is why you should bathe the donkey regularly so that the ones that have hatched can be washed away. Eventually you will reach a stage when the existing eggs have hatched but the adults have been removed before they can lay more eggs.

You may ask your vet to suggest a good anti lice shampoo. If that is unavailable, you can use a baby shampoo that is mild and perfume free. That way, the eyes and the skin of the donkey will not be harmed.

You can follow these steps to bathe your donkey safely:

- Make sure that you use lukewarm water unless the weather is very hot. When you are bathing your donkey, you have to take a lot of time to reassure the animal.
- You will need a lot of watering cans and sprinkler heads in order to hose the donkey down with warm and cold water alternatively.
- You will also need two sponges to clean the face and the ears.
- It is a good idea to have someone along with you to assist you when you are bathing the donkey.
- To start the bath, fill a bucket with warm water. Make sure that you have the right temperature. If the water is too hot or cold, it will startle the donkey.
- The body should be wet all over except for the head and the ears. You must pour the water over the animal slowly and avoid drenching him in one go. If this the first bath, remember that it is a strange sensation for the donkey.
- Take a small amount of the shampoo and massage it onto the body. The more shampoo you use, the harder it will be to rinse it off.
- Begin from the neck and work your way down. Pay attention to the mane, the armpits, the withers and the groin. These are the areas with maximum lice infestation.

- Then wet the face and the areas just behind the ears with a sponge. Cover the eyes with your hand while you do this.
- You can squeeze a small amount of shampoo on the sponge and work it on the skin in these areas.
- Rinse the whole body thoroughly using clean, warm water. You can use a cup or a clean sponge over the ears and the face of the donkey. You must be very careful not to get any water into the eyes of the donkey.
- Dab the body dry with large towels. You will need the smaller ones for the ears and the face.

Once your donkey has been bathed, praise it immensely and reward him/her. You can use a ginger biscuit as a special bath time reward. Make sure that all the grooming tools and the bathing material that you use is washed completely after the bath. That way, you can ensure that it is safe to be used for the next bath.

Remember to keep calm when you do this and take it slow. Never make sudden changes in your interaction with the donkey or you will scare it.

5. Stable maintenance

If you have younger donkeys on your farm, you need to know that they have a very sensitive respiratory system. If you are unable to maintain the stable in a good condition, it will lead to a lot of health issues in the donkey. Here are a few stable management tips that will help you keep the stable clean and tidy.

- **Wear the right clothes:** While you are cleaning the stable, wearing the right clothes can save you a lot of time and can also prevent injuries. Start by wearing gloves that will protect you from blisters. Then, wearing rubber shoes will save you a lot of time that may otherwise be spent on cleaning the shoes.

- **Clear out the area that is to be cleaned:** Get your donkey out of the stable or shelter. The best time to clean the stable is when your donkey is grazing in the pasture. You need to get all the feeding and watering troughs out of the way. If you are unable to get your donkey to stay outside, you can tether it temporarily while you clean up the stall.

- **Get your tools in place:** You will need a large wheelbarrow in order to collect all the muck that you are likely to rake out of the stable of your donkey. A pitchfork or a shovel is also necessary to do a thorough cleaning job with the stable.

- **Dig out the muck:** If the bedding consists of hay, you will need a pitchfork to rake it all out. If you are using sawdust or shavings, you will need a shavings fork. The wet bedding and manure should be removed to ensure that the stable is clean. You can fork everything out into the wheelbarrow. Take out small portions so that it becomes easy for you to push the wheelbarrow around. Choose a dedicated manure pile where you can drop off all the muck you raked out.

- **Even the area:** Once you have removed all the wet bedding and manure, the clean bedding should be spread over the floor just as before. You should make sure that bedding is distributed evenly. Make sure you check the edges to ensure that the middle is not thinner than the sides.

  The new bedding should be fluffed out using the pitchfork. You can even buy compacted shavings if you need to refill the area with clean bedding. The thickness of the bedding will be determined by the flooring and the season. If the weather is cold, you will have to add a thicker layer of bedding. The harder the floor, the thicker the bedding. If the floor is made of rubber matting, for instance, you will not need a thick layer of bedding to go with it.

- **Weekly cleaning schedule:** Having a weekly maintenance schedule can work wonders in reducing the burden of cleaning the area. It is a good idea to remove the wet or soiled bedding on a weekly basis to keep it from getting smelly. Using a stable disinfectant is a good idea. Make sure that the floor is fully dry before you put any bedding back on it.

Once you have completed the cleaning ritual, you need to sweep up any residual manure that may have spilled when cleaning. You can also dust the alleys and doors to get rid of dust and cobwebs. That way, you are assured of thorough cleaning of the stable area.

Always collect the manure and dirt in a designated area. Simply pushing it to the doorway will leave a muddy mess when the rains come in. That may increase the chances of diseases and germs.

If you have a donkey as a pet, you will need to spend a lot of time creating a bond between you and your donkey. Donkeys are gentle creatures that make great companions. You can enrich this experience by trying to understand your pet and building a relationship with it.

6. Understanding the body language

The first step towards building a relationship with your pet is being able to communicate with them. In the case of all pets, verbal communication is the least important tool. What you must focus on mostly is the body language. That will help you figure out the mood and the emotions that your pet is trying to convey. That will make training a lot easier.

a. Approaching a donkey

Communication can be initiated only when you are able to approach your pet confidently without causing any panic or negative experience for either of you. Here are a few tips to approach a donkey properly:

- Make sure that you start slow. Walk towards the donkey slowly and keep the talking to a minimum. The only thing the donkey will focus on is your body and the signals that you are giving out.
- Stop at regular intervals and observe the donkey. Does he want to approach you himself? Or is he trying to get away from you? If he is moving away, you must stand quietly and let him relax.
- After a few moments have elapsed, try to approach the donkey again. Make sure that your hands are lowered. Your donkey may want to smell your hand. That is normal. If you hold the hand up, it might seem like a threat to the donkey, which will think that you are going to strike it.
- When you get close, your donkey might try to sniff at you for sometime. The scent that you emit is one of the most important things for a donkey. This is the first association with a human that the donkey will make. So, be as calm as possible and make sure that you do not startle the animal.

b. Signalling with the ear

The ears of a donkey are a powerful tool of communication. Here are some signals that he/she is trying to give you with the ears:

- If both the ears are facing forward, then the donkey is focusing on something behind you. It may also be trying to understand your movement to figure out where you are trying to go.

- One ear forward and the other back. This is an indication of extreme curiosity. He/she is trying to listen for different sounds in the environment while understanding what you want from him/her.

- Ears to the side, resting flat means that the donkey is relaxed. This is when it is safest to approach the animal.

- Both ears up, facing back. This means that the donkey is aware of some activity that is going on behind it. However, it is still watching you.

- The ears are back and facing down. This is a warning signal that tells you that the donkey is extremely uncomfortable. When you see this ear position, do not approach the donkey at any cost.

b. Signaling with body language

There are a few things that your donkey will do with his/her body after you have successfully approached it. Some may be signs of inviting you while others are telling you to back away.

- The donkey nudges you to tell you to get out of the way. You may be standing in the way of a toy or some food that he/she is eating.

- It makes a nipping action with the mouth. This is a sign of warning. The donkey is telling you that he/she does not approve of you being too close.

- Keeping one leg raised. If the donkey is eating, this means that he/she is fully focused on this activity. You must not approach a donkey in this state, as it may get startled and react in an unexpected manner.

- It pulls at your sleeve. This means that the donkey wants something that you have with you. If this habit is not stopped, it can lead to a painful bite in the future. You must stop this with a strong "No". The voice must be loud and abrupt.

- He/she rests his/her head on your shoulder. This is a sign that the donkey is very comfortable in your presence. A donkey in this state is comfortable with you approaching it.

- He/she turns around and places his/her hind towards you. This is a sign that he/she is extremely nervous. When the donkey does this, do not pet the animal. It might be getting ready to kick the person approaching. This can lead to severe injuries if you get too close to the animal.

- Switching of the tail. This is a signal that the donkey is clearly annoyed by something. You must look around when it does this. If you cannot find anything around you, reexamine your action and movement. If it is too swift or sudden, your donkey will not be too comfortable.

c. How you can use words
While it is true that donkeys do not respond first to verbal communication, it is not obsolete. The tone of your voice is very important and not so much the words that you use.

- Keeping the tone uniform during a certain movement allows your donkey to read what it means. For instance, if you use the word no regularly in a certain tone, it understands that you are not pleased with something.

- The level of the voice is important. If you keep the voice soft and low, it can have a rather calming effect on the donkey.

Remember, while words are not really a method of communicating with animals, the tone is universal. But, without any control on your body language and the energy that you are emitting, the tone of your voice cannot help you much when it comes to dealing with creatures that belong to another species. The cues that you give to the animal are of utmost importance.

2. Training the donkey
Training a donkey is not very different from training a horse. The major difference that you may notice is in the attitude and instinct of the animal. That will change your approach in various situations. The techniques, however, remain the same.

a. Imprinting
With a young foal, imprinting can have a lot of benefits. This is where you get the animal used to your touch, your voice, your smell and your energy. These things are usually taught to a foal by its mother. This will shape the character when it is older.

If you want him/her to be trainable, you need to make sure that you teach it to be willing from the time it is born. You can even ensure that you pick a female that is very calm in her temperament. When she gives birth to a young foal, she will teach it to do the same. On the other hand, if the jennet is difficult to handle, you may have trouble handling her foal.

When you begin to imprint the foal, have the goal clear. Basically, you need to know what attitude you want it to develop. Adopt the right approaching techniques and ensure that you provide it with a lot of patience and calmness. That is what it will learn from you.

If you respect the foal, you can demand respect from him/her. Set limitations with its behavior. If the foal was in a herd, the first thing that it is taught is to respect space. This is what you must try to teach without being too overbearing. If the foal kicks, bites or misbehaves, you can give it a sharp pat on the side of the rump or the mouth.

At the same time, when the foal displays good behavior, do not forget to give it a good reward. That will foster a relationship between you that will last for a really long time.

b. Keep it fun

If learning becomes threatening to the donkey, it will learn very little. Make sure that there is a good balance between work and play. The more fun you make it, the more your donkey will want to be around you. Donkeys have an innate need to serve and please.

Never rush the response with a donkey. If you have trained a horse before, you must not expect the same rate of response from the donkey. With horses, a quick response is the norm. However, the bright side of training a donkey is that while response is slow, the memory and retention is much higher than in a horse.

c. Basics first

Whether you are training a foal or an adult, the one thing that you must keep in mind is to start from the basics. You will begin with imprinting and then take it to the basic routines.

The first thing that you will do is to put on a halter correctly. You can ask the ranch that you bought the donkey from to assist you with this. Once you know that the donkey is not bothered by the removing and putting on of the halter, you can proceed to tether it. After the halter has been placed, find a secure post to tether it to.

Leave him/her after tying him/her and come back after a few minutes. Then untie it and say the words, "Come". He/she may not step forward immediately. If that occurs, tie it again and leave. Try this every ten minutes. The moment your donkey steps forward with you, give it a treat and praise generously.

Stroking a donkey on the neck and the shoulder will be appreciated a lot. You can even stroke the ears and the chest. You can try a few more steps, but don't force him to respond immediately. Try a few steps the first day and a few more in the days that follow.

Once you are able to lead the donkey easily, walk it around the farm. You can introduce him/her to things like machines that may scare him/her when you begin the training process. A calm introduction will prevent fear in the future. Make sure you give your donkey a lot of rewards as you walk along. The more you reward, the easier to lead.

Once you are able to walk, you can set up tiny obstacles or even choose obstacles around your farm and pasture. The best options are logs, bridges and tires. The donkey may be unwilling to negotiate these obstacles initially. However, it will try when coaxed. Use a short lead and stand very close to the head. Then say the word, "come" to pull it forward. The moment your donkey is able to move one foot over the obstacle, stop right there and reward. When he/she proceeds with the next foot, reward him/her again and so on. This obstacle course should be slow and easy. Don't rush through it.

What you need to bear in mind is that the donkey will not walk straight on the obstacle, but may tend to become a little crooked. Then, you will walk in front of him. Be directly in front, hold his halter on either side and make him walk in a straight line.

The way to know if the basic training is successful is if the donkey is able to walk with you on a slack lead easily. If it is resisting, be consistent and persistent in training. Keep stopping and starting until he/she is able to walk with you on a loose leash. That will also help you control the speed at which it walks. You can make him/her jog and trot on command with a loose leash.

The next way to know is that the donkey will stand in place with the lead and halter. While you brush him, he will stand still and stay completely calm.

b. Advanced training
Donkeys can learn pretty much any verbal command that you may want to teach a dog. However, there are some commands that will be beneficial to the donkey and also to the owner when taught correctly.

Whoa

This is the command that you will use when you want the donkey to stop. When you want it to stop just stop walking yourself and use the command "Whoa". If he complies, you can reward him. This is an important command if your donkey is about to attack a family pet, is going to run into a fence or is in any dangerous situation.

Over

You want to train the donkey to move over or turn around. This is a little hard, as you have to approach from the front and nudge him/her to do it. Unless your animal has complete trust in you, it will view this as a predatory move and may attack. For ease sake, we will continue to refer to the donkey as "he", however everything also applies to a female donkey.

Take the donkey into a training pen and let it relax and get familiar with the area. Then, step towards the shoulder and pull the head towards you. You can tap him on the flank and give him the verbal command of "Move over". You must not move with your body unless the donkey is very reluctant to move.

The first thing the donkey needs to learn is hindquarter control. That will only come when you are gentle. Take it one step at a time. If he crosses over the offside hind, give him a reward and encourage him to step more. For the first time you can stop at two steps. You can ask for few more steps with each session.

The next step is to get the shoulders away from you. This is harder, as the front feet are usually glued hard on the floor. Hold the side of the halter and ask it to move over again. This time, give him a firmer tap. Use your body weight to bring him around if he does not comply immediately.

You can repeat this three times. If he does not comply, then you can give him a sharp tap on the shoulder once. He may just step over by surprise. That is when you will reward him very generously.

Back

The final and most important command is back. You will have to use the lead in the left hand and pull it back in a downward direction. Then release it while you say the command, "back". Normally, a donkey will step back. If it doesn't, you can use the right hand to push at the middle of the chest and release. This works best when you use a single finger. You have to push him quite hard to get him to move the first time.

The moment he steps back, pet him and reward him. Repeat this not more than three times and complete the session. You can keep increasing the response each time.

With every verbal command, you can try three repetitions each time. Do not force him to do any more than that, as he can get a little aggressive. Once he is able to comply well, you can improve the training by teaching him commands such as lunge. These commands take a lot of patience and will require your donkey to have some trust in you to perform it perfectly.

Never train the donkey in a hurry. You should be able to spend a lot of time together and make this a fun and enjoyable experience for the both of you. Fast-forwarding training is never going to get you the response you want from the donkey.

d. Riding the donkey

All of the commands mentioned above were with respect to handling the donkey by the halter. Now, the next thing that you want to be able to do is ride the donkey. First, you must have all the verbal commands in place, especially whoa and trot. If his ground drive during the walk is easy, you are ready to mount him. That is only possible if he is a donkey that is large enough to ride.

Get him used to the idea of mounting. Mount from one side and dismount from the other and watch his reaction. If he is able to remain calm, then you have the opportunity to stay on his back for a while. After you sit on his back, hold a treat to his mouth and encourage him to move his head around a little to get the treat from you. While doing so, you can even gently tug at the halter and rein on the sides. This will give you the benefit of a light brindle when you begin to walk him. Your donkey is fairly ready to move ahead with you still aboard. This will require an assistant initially.

Let the person with you lead the donkey forward. Remember that both of you have to give the "come" or "walk" command. To give the donkey a cue, you will have to squeeze the legs around the body. That is when your assistant will lead him on. A riding crop might be necessary if he does not comply at first.

After every few steps, use the "whoa" command. If he stops on command, give him a reward. Even if he has only walked two steps, it is a significant mark of progress. Continue this lesson until your donkey has finished one complete rotation of the stable one way. Always remind him to stop with a "whoa" command. If your donkey is good with the back up command, you can ask him to do this as well.

You can give your donkey a cue to stop as well. As you say "whoa", pull the reins gently. That will become a habit even without the verbal cue.

Back up can be taught to the donkey by pulling the reins down and back. In case he does not comply with this in the first few attempts, you have the option of getting your assistant to push him back as you had done previously while teaching him the command. When you are pushing him back with the reins, watch his reaction. If he is jutting his head forward, it means that he is not happy doing it. If you persist too much, he may have a negative response.

Remember that donkeys learn quite differently from horses. The response might be slower and a little frustrating at first. All you need to do is stay in tune with the person who is assisting you. Be very careful not to confuse the donkey.

The next thing that you want to teach him is to trot with you aboard. This is not the easiest thing to do but it can be achieved. Riding with a donkey is a great idea because of the temperament of the animal. He is less likely to get startled and bolt off. They are also willing to work with you for long periods of time after they have been trained. That said, if you have smaller sized donkeys, they tend to have the personality of a pony and will try their best to get away with stuff often.

Strength is the most important quality of a donkey. They are able to carry some large weights on their body without even flinching. They are also a lot more surefooted, although there have been cases of stumbling in the past. The one thing you need to remember with the donkey is that you must never lean forward, as the speed picks up as it would do with a horse. This will throw him off balance. To be on the safer side, you must try to get the donkey to move at fast speeds only when the route is somewhat leveled.

7. What all donkeys can do

You can have a lot of fun with donkeys and they are great utility creatures as well. Once they are trained, they can perform a variety of tasks depending upon the breed that you are handling and the physical traits of each individual donkey.

The personality of a donkey is quite astonishing. They have the best pet qualities if you are able to spend a few hours training them and trying to get them used to you and your energy. Besides the fact that they can be wonderful companions, donkeys can perform several tasks routinely at the pasture. Here are a few things that you can use your donkey for:

- **Sheep protection:** This task is usually presented to geldings and jennets. Jacks can become too aggressive with the sheep. You can introduce your donkey to the herd using temporary fences. After a while, the single donkey will form a bond with the herd. When this happens, the donkey will protect the herd from any canine predator.

  If you have a pasture with sheep that are free ranging, then this is a huge advantage. The reason why people prefer to keep donkeys over guard dogs is that donkeys feed just like the sheep and you can have them feed and live together. With dogs you have to invest in their food separately.

Donkeys can even live in the same area as the sheep. In the case of any danger, the donkey will also raise an alarm that will alert the sheep. In case of a predator attack, donkeys are known to chase the predator and trample it. This is not a common occurrence with miniature donkeys, as they are too small to go after the predator.

- **Halter breaking:** A standard-sized donkey will also halter break the younger donkeys after they have been trained. The trained or older donkey will sport a collar that is connected to the younger donkey's halter. You can leave them out in the pasture under supervision.

Lead training is an unpleasant task and when you let the donkey train a younger one, the latter will not associate you with the negative experience. You can get any breed of donkey to perform this task for you. They are naturally attuned to training younger donkeys.

- **Foal companionship:** During the weaning stage, a donkey can make a wonderful companion to foals. Let the donkey run around the pasture with the mare before you wean the foal. Then, when you are weaning the foal, you can leave the donkey with him.

A donkey makes for a very calm companion. It also makes them very steady mentally. You will notice that the foal will actually turn to the donkey for comfort. That reduces the stress caused by separation from the dam. Most donkeys are comfortable around people. This trait is also transferred to the donkey. So, when you bring home a donkey companion for a foal, you reduce the stress of separation and also make the foal people-friendly.

- **Stable companion:** This role is similar to providing companionship to the foal. Donkeys will actually take on the responsibility of improving the well being of other animals. If you have a nervous horse in your stable, you can introduce him to a donkey that will make for a wonderful pasture and stall mate. You can also introduce the donkey as a companion to a horse that is recovering from surgery or trauma. This is very useful for racehorses that need to develop that calmness after an injury.

The best donkey for this purpose is the miniature donkey, as they do not take up much space but provide the same amount of positive energy to the animal.

- **Riding programs for the handicapped** - Time and again, donkeys have proved that they can have a very positive effect on children and people who are disabled. In most parts of England, the donkey is promoted as an animal that can be in riding programs for the physically challenged.

  Since they are smaller in size and have a much calmer disposition, they are easy for them to ride. Donkeys are very thoughtful and can be extremely affectionate towards these individuals. If you can train the donkey to allow people to ride him, you will see that they develop the most special bond with the people in these programs.

- **Working donkey:** There are several jobs that your donkey can carry out. The most common ones are riding, packing and recreational purposes. Many backpackers will have a donkey accompany them on their adventures. Since they are able to carry heavy loads, they are ideal for these trips. The best thing about donkeys is that they can walk at human pace quite easily. They can carry farm material such as fencing, firewood, trash and other items. This transporting can be done with the help of panniers that are convenient in comparison to carts.

- **Mule breeding:** This is one of the most important functions of a donkey. We will learn all about breeding in the following chapters. The best breed of donkeys for mule breeding is the mammoth breed. You can even employ standard sized donkeys for this purpose if you have smaller sized horses.

Bonding with your donkey can be very fulfilling and a lot of fun. However, you will have to dedicate a lot of time and ensure that you are patient with your animal. They retain information for long periods of time and can become a great helping hand in your farm and pasture.

8. Toys for the donkey

While donkeys have often been labeled as stupid and dull, they are very good thinkers. They need a lot of mental stimulation in order to remain healthy. Now, it is easy for your donkey to get bored. If you have a donkey that is bored, he will pick up just about anything to play with.

In order to keep your donkey happy, make sure that you have ample toys for him to play with. When they are able to keep themselves amused, they will give up habits like cribbing on the barn and fence. If you have a male donkey, you have to be particularly concerned about the mental stimulation, as they love to play hard. They can build up a lot of energy that is channeled in a negative manner when they do not have ways to release it.

Here are some toy ideas for your donkey. They are inexpensive but will be loved by your pet:

- Empty cardboard boxes. You can even put treats inside these boxes and watch the donkey have a great time.

- Milk jugs or water jugs made from plastic. Fill this with some colored water to amuse the donkey.

- An old garden hose. Remove the metal ends to provide the animal with a safe toy.

- Cotton rope or cloth tied in knots. This is quite similar to the tug toy that you would provide a dog.

- Inner tube of the bicycle or a bicycle tire. Make sure any metal fill that is present is removed.

- Traffic cones that are brightly colored. These are the most popular toys as far as donkeys are concerned.

- Large sized balls that the donkey can pick up with the mouth and kick around. A football is a great option.

When you have the right toys, you can make your donkey very happy. A happy donkey is also very obedient. Playing is one of the best forms of exercise for your donkey. The more they are able to release energy, the calmer they are going to be in the long run.

Chapter 4: Breeding Donkeys

Breeding a donkey requires you to understand the health of the jennets and stallions in your stable. The first thing that you need to think about is whether you want to breed your donkey or not. If you are not able to manage the demands of a pregnant mare, it is best that you opt for other choices.

1. Do you breed or not?

This is the first question that you should ask yourself. Here are a few tips that you need to keep in mind when you have a mature jennet or stallion:

- The jennet or stallion should be examined thoroughly. Make a note of any conformation fault that might be obvious. It is best to have your donkey examined thoroughly by a vet. In case of an older jennet over ten years of age, make sure you discuss the possible outcomes of breeding the animal. In older jennets, foal rejection is a common problem if they have not been able to have a successful delivery in the past.

- The reproductive tract of the donkey should be checked to ensure that it is healthy. Even if your donkey looks perfect from the outside, he or she may have underlying issues.

- Make sure that the donkey you want to breed is perfectly trained. They need halter training and should be easy for you to catch. This is especially important with jennets that may need your assistance when giving birth.

- Visit the owner of the jack or jennet who you plan to mate your pet with. You must understand the methods that will be used, especially if you have a jennet that you are sending to a jack owner. You can also talk about the history of your pet's mate, the breeding habits and other details. You can ask for a health certificate and a Coggins test paper for your donkey's possible mate.

- It is necessary to get the hooves of your jennet trimmed and ensure that she is dewormed. You must also provide your donkey with the necessary vaccination before breeding.

- If you are breeding your jennet with a stallion, it is good to know if it is a mule jack or a jennet jack. While there is no physical difference, you will see that they are drastically different in terms of behavior. A mule jack will have the traits of a horse but will look like a donkey. So there are chances that he will attack the jennet. She may be bitten and kicked and it is not easy to put an end to a confrontation like this. The result is that your jennet will be petrified and may not even allow you to approach her after that.

- Evaluate the behavior of the animal that your pet will be bred with. You have to check the conformation, the disposition, temperament and obedience of the animal in these cases. You have to take into account serious things like the height of the two animals and the compatibility before allowing them to be bred.

- Avoid breeding your donkey in the winter and fall months. This is an option only when you have a heated barn that you can use to foal the mare in cold weathers. The mare will take about 11-14 months to deliver the foal. So it is essential that you get your timing right. Ideally, foaling must occur in between April and August for the most conducive environment for the donkey and the easiest foaling experience for you.

If you take into consideration all the points mentioned above, you should be able to provide an environment for optimum development of the foal. In addition to that, you will also have healthy parents after the breeding process is complete.

2. Donkey breeding methods

There are different ways to breed donkeys. The breeding methods for donkeys are quite similar to the breeding methods of horses. So, if you are successful in finding a suitable mate for your donkey, here are three options that you can choose from:

a. Pasture breeding

This is a suitable method when you have a herd of donkeys with one jack and several jennets. This is a natural breeding situation that is probably the simplest option available.

Disadvantages

- If the jack is not healthy, he will be unable to breed all the mares in your pasture

- If one or more of the jennets or the jack himself is aggressive, there is a chance of injury

- The foals in the herd run the risk of being injured. In many cases the jack will try to kill the foal if he is male too

- The risk of being infected is always higher, as the breeding method is not entirely in your control

- You have no sure shot way of determining when the jennets were bred and as a result, the foaling dates become unpredictable.

b. In hand breeding

This training method is used when the jack is being controlled by the handler and the jennet is in a breeding stall. With this method you need to take a lot of care when handling the animal. You will also need additional facilities in order to breed the donkeys. In most cases, the jack is a slow breeder and you will have to tease the mare constantly.

Advantages
- The controlled environment means that the jack or jennet is at a lesser risk of being injured.

- You can even place the foal near the jennet to ensure that she is not anxious about the well being of her offspring.

- The risk of infection is greatly reduced, as the jack and the jennet can be tested and disinfected before they are allowed to breed.

- You can make a record of the exact breeding date, which also means that you can adequately prepare yourself for the foaling season.

c. Artificial insemination

The semen of a jack is collected in order to inseminate single or multiple jennets that are ready to breed. The biggest disadvantage with his method is that most breeders and owners cannot afford to hire a technician who can work with the donkey. You will also have to study extensively and complete a course if you plan to have the donkey artificially inseminated at the stable. The equipment required can also be very expensive.

Advantages:

- The risk of injury is significantly lowered
- You can breed several jennets at once

- You can breed to obtain desirable qualities in the offspring.

Donkeys mature quite slowly and young jacks can be precocious when they are younger. In the case of the female, the first heat cycle is experienced when they are a year old. However, allowing your donkeys to breed before they are three years of age is not a good idea.

If the jennet is not mature, the foal may have several deformities. In addition to that, the gestation period for donkeys is really long and taxing. This can lead to permanent damage of the muscular and the skeletal system in the dam. The younger jennets are also not mentally mature to make good mothers.

It is necessary to choose the jennet and the jack wisely. Then you will have a beautiful, long eared, fuzzy foal in the following foaling season.

3. Foaling a jennet
Usually a change of season means that the foaling season is around the corner. If you plan your breeding well, you will mostly have to worry about foaling during spring each year. The last quarter of your mare's pregnancy is a waiting game because the gestation period may wary between 11-14 months.

a. Healthy foaling tips
To make sure that the mare is healthy, here are a few pregnancy tips that you must follow:

- The donkey should receive good exercise
- She must not be allowed to perform any hard labor
- Consult your vet to put a hoof care program in place
- Deworming the mare is a must before she is ready to give birth
- Provide the medicine recommended by the vet during the last quarter of your mare's pregnancy.

A change in diet must only be made when the donkey is in the last quarter of the gestation period. This is when the fetus will make maximum development. Feeding your mare excessively before this stage will lead to obesity and other fat-related issues.

You can increase the feed from the last quarter up to the third month after foaling. This is when she will need more nutrition in order to produce enough milk for the foal.

During this phase you will have to increase the vitamin, calcium, phosphorous and mineral levels in the food. This helps the dam cope with the physical stress that is caused by the gestation period. If you are unsure of what to feed your donkey, you can consult your vet or an equine nutritionist. The diet plays a crucial role during this time for your mare. Make sure that you have the breeding dates in place for your mare. That will help you foal her appropriately and also prepare for the foaling stage. Make a note of the progression towards foaling and the changes that you see in the mare. This will give you a good idea for the next foaling season about what you can expect.

On average, you can expect to foal your mare when she is in the 12th month of the gestation period in most cases. In some cases, the donkey may be ready much earlier. Therefore, you need to remain alert about the signs that your mare shows about being ready to give birth.

b. Signs that the dam is ready

- You will notice that the udder will enlarge gradually about a month before the birth. When the birthing date comes closer, the udder of the donkey will become enlarged and will stay enlarged.

- Just a few days before birth, this enlargement will go right up to the teats.

- You will see a waxy secretion over the teats, which forms a cap. This is an indication that the foal is due in 48 hours. Some of the pregnant jennets may drip milk. Remember that you must not milk a jennet during this phase at any cost.

- The pelvic ligaments will get softer, leaving a groove on the either side of the spinal cord. It is a noticeable groove from the loin towards the tail. If it is maiden jennet, you may not notice this. In the case of a winter foaling, you will be unable to notice this because of a thick coat that develops during the winter months.

- In the last week, you will notice extreme softening of the vulva. Gradually, this region elongates as the date of birthing approaches.

- If you notice that the vulva is swollen, then the birth of the foal is just few hours away.

- A few days before birthing, the foal will become very reserved and will change her demeanor towards other animals. She will just like to stand alone and will even ignore her companions.

- In the case of donkeys, the foal will turn inside the womb. That is when the mare will experience a lot of discomfort. She will become restless and will walk around, get up and sit down several times and will also appear thinner. In some cases, birth will occur on the same day. In others, you will have to wait for a day or more for the foaling to occur.

- Just before the foal is born, the tail is lifted away from the body and one side. She may even urinate or pass some soft feces.

You will notice various signs of foaling in a jennet. You have to be really observant, as there is no fixed time of birth. They may foal anytime in the night or day. It is essential that you keep a fenced corral ready for foaling.

You can also use a clean box stall for the same. Make sure that that foaling does not occur near barbed wires, among the herd, near streams, etc., as it can be disastrous for the new born.

c. Preparing for foaling
- Watch out for the signs of foaling and have your jennet in the foaling box at least one or two weeks before the due date.

- Make sure that the foaling box is cleaned fully to prevent any infection. Have a thick bedding of wheat or barley straw before you provide her with access.

- From the time the jennet is placed in the foaling box, it must be cleaned on a daily basis.

- There are chances that your jennet will go off the feed before foaling. This may seem stressful to you but it is completely normal. The jennet is only trying to cleanse the digestive system before delivering the foal.

d. Arrival of the foal
The birthing process begins with a lot of restlessness. She will sit down and get up several times and will pace up and down. Then you will see these signs, which shows you that the foal is ready:

- The water bag protrudes from the cervix, which is fully dilated by now. Then, the amniotic fluid is released into the vagina to lubricate the passage for the foal.

- You will notice extreme strain in the jennet's body as she pushes the foal through. The forefeet are the first part to appear.

- The feet will be pointed downward and as the jennet pushes, you will see that the nose of the foal appears, resting on the forelimbs. You must not try to pull unless there is an obvious issue.

- The licking reflex is seen in the jennet much before the foal is actually born.

- After about 20 minutes of straining, if the only thing that appears is the front feet and you do not see signs of the nose, call the vet. You must never see the red placental mass being released before the foal appears.

- When the neck comes out of the vagina, you will see the foal moving the head around. This will break the membrane surrounding its body.

- In case the membrane does not break, you will have to tear it open and also wipe the nostrils of the foal to make sure that it does not asphyxiate.

- As soon as the membrane is broken, you will see the nostrils flare. It will also show the sucking reflex.

- When the birth is complete, you must never try to cut the navel cord. It will be broken by the jennet as soon as she gets up. It may even snap when the foal tries to get on its feet.

- You can imprint the foal if you have a good relationship with the jennet right from this time.

e. After the foal is born
- As soon as the jennet is on her feet, she will lick the foal. This is a very important step with first time jennets especially, because it stimulates the instinct of motherhood. This also helps keep the newborn warm.

- After about half an hour, the jennet will get on her feet to expel the placenta.

- If this does not happen in 6-8 hours, you must ask for assistance. Any placenta that is retained can lead to infections.

- After the naval cord breaks, you will have to dip the stump on the foal in 5 percent iodine solution to make sure that there is no infection. Continue this for 5 days after the birth of the foal to make sure that there is no risk of infection.

- The colostrum or the first milk is very essential for the foal as it allows it to stay immune. In the case of first time jennets, nursing should be assisted. You will have to hold the jennet or have her tied when the foal is nursing.

- The first manure or the meconium is important to watch out for. When the foal is trying to get on to his feet to nurse, he will pass the first hard pellets. In case the foal is unable to pass this manure in within 24 hours or if you see signs of straining without the manure passing, it will have to be stimulated with mineral oil. Make sure you consult your vet for this purpose.

- If the pasture that your foal is on is deficient in selenium, you will have to administer a selenium injection in the first 24 hours of his birth. This is essential to make sure that he does not develop white muscle disease. A booster is provided after two weeks as a precautionary measure.

- Although the donkey foal looks really robust with his thick coat, he will need a good shelter for the first four weeks after birth. Getting drenched or getting too cold will make them develop conditions like pneumonia and bronchitis. This is usually fatal for the foal. If the foal does get drenched, towel dry him and take him to the jennet until he is fully dry.

f. Weaning in foals
- When the foal is about 2 weeks old, he will automatically begin to feed on the jennet's fodder. This is when he is ready to be fed in a separate enclosure called a creep.

- It has been noted that a foal that is fed in a creep develops and grows much faster. Even the quality of development is much better in creep fed foals.

- You can feed him close to 18% of commercial foal food to make his growth optimum.

- When the foal is about 9 days old, you will notice diarrhea. This is not something that you need to worry about, as it will disappear without having any effect on the foal. If the problem persists and you see that the foal looks sick, you have to consult your vet to check if he has been nursing normally.

- Weaning completely takes place when the foal is 6 months old. Until then, creep feeding is the best option.

- Unless there is an emergency, you must never attempt to wean a foal before he is 3 months old. This will reduce the chance of survival in the foal if he does not get the appropriate care. You will also have several psychological and physiological issues with these foals.

After about 10 days of foaling, there are chances that your jennet will go back into heat. This is not a good time to breed her, however. The development of the fetus or even the chances of conception are very low during this phase.

The reproductive system of the jennet is still under recovery. In addition to that, her focus is mostly on nursing the new foal. She will become extremely upset when you take her to a jack.

The jennet is ready to be bred around the third heat cycle. She will be a lot more receptive to a jack as the foal is able to stay in a separate pen or stall.

If you are purely interested in breeding your jennet, you will not achieve one foal every year. This is because of factors like the recovery period and also the fact that the gestation period is long. So, logically, you can expect only about two foals in a span of three years.

In order to improve the quality of life of the jennet, you must plan to breed her every alternate year. Since the donkey has a long life span, this is a practical schedule to have. Plan to foal the jennet in spring, as the quality of grass is also high for the foal.

Chapter 5: Transporting Donkeys

This is a very important factor in raising donkeys. People often believe that horses are the only equines that require transportation. However, from time to time, you may have to transport your donkey from one farm to another or even haul them to another state or city for several reasons, like moving out, for instance. To reduce stress and discomfort, this chapter will give you some important tips on managing your donkey's transportation.

1. Transportation guidelines

There are several guidelines in the UK and the USA when it comes to transporting livestock. Adhering to that is a mandate when it comes to private animals as well. These guidelines have been put into place to make sure that the welfare of the animal is maintained when transporting. In case you are transporting the animal abroad, the vet will have to provide appropriate health certificates.

a. Loading the donkey

For anyone who is transporting donkeys for the first time, loading the animal presents itself as the biggest challenge. Here are a few tips that can make it easier:

- Never rush the donkey. When you try to push a donkey that is hesitant into doing something, it usually spells trouble. No trick like luring him with treats or food will work. The best you can do is use a long lead that you can secure on a ring in the front of the trailer.

- Before you get the donkey loaded in, tether him to the ring. You will need two people to get him into the trailer. One who will actually lead him into the trailer and another who can stop him from going backwards.

- Make sure that the ring is secured properly. You see, a donkey can be extremely stubborn, so if he decides not to enter and just back up, you will need the support of the lead.

In some cases, the donkey will enter the trailer only half way and freeze. This is when just two feet are in the trailer. In that case, you do not have to make it a big deal. Stay relaxed and move around calmly. Don't make too many noises like opening and closing doors, as it will make the donkey very suspicious and will prevent it from entering the trailer at all.

- Food must never be used to lure the donkey. It is advisable to use treats when the donkey enters. Only if you are not familiar with the donkey can you use grass or grains to get him into the trailer.

In order to get the donkey into a trailer, you need a lot of patience. Making the trailer a place that the donkey will feel comfortable in is the first step towards getting him in.

Place a lot of bedding inside and keep the trailer clean. There should not be any flies or insects. Having a well-ventilated trailer is crucial if it is a warm day.

Park your trailer in such a way that the donkey cannot escape from the sides. The lower the ramp, the easier it is. If this is your first attempt at transporting your donkey, make sure that you place him in the trailer and take small trips before you actually go on a long drive.

b. Recommendations for transportation
- Use a basic trailer that is towed by a vehicle. Avoid journey durations beyond 8 hours. If necessary, you can take breaks in between.

- If you are using a trailer that is borrowed, make sure that you check the floor, ramp, catches and lights for safety.

- Don't forget to check the towing capacity of the trailer. That will help you plan the number of donkeys you can transport.

- The trailer must comply with all the legal requirements such as the cables, the brake, the tire, spare wheels and the registration plate.

- For journeys that are longer than 8 hours, there is a specially designed lorry. You can even choose a train journey or ferry if available.

- When travelling long distances, make sure that the donkey has ample space, food, water and ventilation.

- The donkey will use most of his energy trying to maintain his balance when traveling, so ensure that you drive as slowly as you can to reduce the stress caused to the animal. Pay attention to the acceleration, breaking and cornering.

- Make sure you choose a route that is smooth and can keep the journey continuous.

- The journey must be planned with a lot of care to make sure that you do not have any delays due to traffic. Any ventilation in the trailer occurs only when the vehicle keeps moving forward.

- Make plans to travel during the colder months of the year. Travelling in heat or scorching summers can be taxing for you and the donkey.

- Make sure that that the bedding you have in the trailer will absorb the urine and feces completely. If it is not thick enough, you will have to clean it out frequently.

- Rubber matting is the best option when it comes to bedding to make it comfortable. You can add shavings to increase the absorption in the trailer.

- If you compromise on the bedding, the air quality in the trailer also reduces, making the journey very uncomfortable for the donkey.

- The box must be cleaned thoroughly at the end of the journey to prepare it for the upcoming one.

- Never carry hay nets outside the trailer or the vehicle. They will absorb all the emissions of the vehicle and will become unhealthy to use with your donkey.

- A fully charged mobile phone must be available at all times with the number of the contact person at the destination, emergency services in case of a breakdown, your vet and other relevant contacts.

- If it is possible to take an assistant with you who is familiar with your donkeys, do so.

- Any drinking water or bucket must be carried in the towing vehicle. Putting this in the trailer can lead to unwanted spilling.

- The passport of the donkey must be carried in case you are stopped by the authorities or if your donkey needs medical attention.

- A spare leash and collar is a must, as you may have a breakage and other issues.

- A fluorescent waistcoat and torch is mandatory if you are travelling at night.

- Minor injuries are quite common when travelling. Carry a first aid kit that has all the contents mentioned in the following chapter.

- Your vehicle must have adequate fuel before you begin the journey.

c. Checking on the donkey
There are a few things that you can do to make sure that your donkey is not stressed when travelling:

- Maximum stress occurs when the donkey is being loaded and unloaded. You can prevent this stress by planning these steps and carrying them out with helpers who have good experience.

- Carry haylage and damp hay for a long journey so that you can feed the donkey when you are resting.

- The donkey must be checked on every four hours without fail. You must offer water every 4 hours at least.

- Make sure you do not bandage the donkey when travelling. This can lead to overheating.

- The donkey should be fit to travel. You can check with your vet to ensure that your donkey can travel long distances.

d. Seeking veterinary help
Make sure you call a vet if you see any of these signs:

- Reduced appetite
- Nasal discharge or respiratory disorder
- Sickness
- Lameness
- If you are transporting a pregnant dam
- A young foal that is still sucking
- A young foal less than 1 week old.

e. Getting a passport for the donkey

In most parts of the UK and Europe, travelling donkeys will require a passport. It is the job of the owner to make sure that their donkey has a passport that is valid when making plans for long distance travel. Here are some tips to get a passport for your equine:

- Contact the Department of Environment for Food and Rural Affairs or an equivalent authority in your country to check for authorities that issue passports to donkeys.

- Make sure that you fill out all the relevant paperwork after you have filed the application.

- You will have to provide details like the distinctive markings and a description of your donkey.

- It is mandatory to have the donkey micro-chipped. You can consult your vet for this.

- Your veterinary surgeon will have to provide a silhouette drawing of the donkey for proper identification.

- You can even sign a statement that says that your donkey cannot enter the human food chain.

- If you do not own the donkey but are the keeper, you will be logged as keeper in the passport.

- In case your keeper changes, make sure that your passport is updated accordingly.

Passports are mandatory and failure to have one when travelling makes you liable for a fine and also prosecution.

f. Points to remember

There are a few points that you need to keep in mind when travelling with a donkey:

- If your donkey has any respiratory issues, it may worsen when travelling. Travelling leads to a lot of breathing issues in donkeys.
- The food and water intake of the donkey may reduce significantly when you are travelling. This should be restored in a couple of days.

- Always have a map handy in case you have to change routes if the one that you have chosen is stressful to the donkey.

- Any pre-existing health condition might increase due to the stress of travelling.

- Consult your vet about proper travelling precautions.

With these simple tips in mind, you are ready to travel safely with the donkey. The primary goal is to make sure that you need to reduce stress and anxiety in the animal as much as possible.

Chapter 6: Common illnesses of Donkeys

Taking care of your donkey's health is your first responsibility as a pet owner. Now, the biggest concern with donkeys is that they are extremely stoic. That means that they are experts in covering up illnesses, so you have to be very attentive to notice the smallest deviation from normal.

In this chapter, you will come across the term zootonic quite often. This refers to diseases that can be transmitted from animals to humans.

We will talk about the symptoms of the diseases and understand the best ways to prevent them from occurring or from being transmitted.

1. Identifying a sick donkey

The biggest challenge faced by donkey owners is that they will show almost no signs of illness in the initial stages of contracting a disease.

There are three signs that you must watch out for:

- Sudden loss in appetite
- Depression
- Dullness

The last two are quite hard to understand because donkeys are, by nature, very docile and reserved creatures. You may often mistake depression for general behavior. This is why you need to make sure that you interact with your donkey regularly. Even the slightest deviation from normal behavior indicates that you need to see a vet immediately.

2. Common illnesses in donkeys

There are some diseases that are very common in horses and donkeys. You need to be very careful about identifying these conditions and helping the animal recover at the earliest. If you have a herd, especially, you need to be careful that the diseases do not spread from one animal to another.

Tetanus or lockjaw

This condition occurs if the skin or the hoof is damaged. The microorganism causing tetanus lives in the intestines of the donkey and can affect a donkey that has been injured or has had surgery. If your donkey develops this condition, it is usually fatal.

Prevention

- Provide an annual tetanus toxoid vaccine
- If the animal has had surgery, provide a tetanus anti-toxin injection within 24 hours.

Rabies

A donkey with rabies will become aggressive. There have been reports of accidents that have proved fatal to humans. This is a zootonic disease that often affects the brain of the animal. If your donkey is bitten by a rabid skunk, dog, raccoon, fox or other animal, and if a human is bitten by an affected donkey, they can develop the condition. Treatment is a long process that lasts for several weeks. A rabid horse will also succumb to the condition.

Prevention:
- Get the animal an annual vaccine
- A brooding mare should be vaccinated just before breeding.

Encephalomyelitis

This condition is also called EEE or Easter Equine Encephalomyelitis, WEE or Western Equine Encephalomyelitis and Venezuelan Equine Encephalomyelitis or VEE.

This is another zootonic disease that affects the spinal cord and the brain of the affected animal. The condition is normally transmitted from rodents and birds to equines by mosquitos. VEE is transmitted to human beings and not EEE or WEE. A horse affected by this condition usually succumbs or will have a severely damaged nervous system.

Prevention:
- Annual vaccination for WEE and EEE
- Vaccination for VEE should be provided as per the recommendation of your vet.

West Nile Virus

This is another zootonic disease that affects the brain of the animal. It is transmitted from birds and rodents to the equines by mosquitos. Horses that are affected will die or will develop permanent damage to the nervous system.

Prevention
- Annual vaccination

Equine influenza

The donkey develops a high fever with these symptoms:
- Depression
- Cough
- Weakness

The appetite of the donkey is affected and he may stop eating completely. Usually the donkey will recover in about 3 days. However, symptoms will be seen for almost 6 months. In extreme cases, it is fatal to the donkey.

Prevention
- Have your donkey vaccinated every 3-6 months

Rhino Virus Abortion

This is a strain of herpes virus that commonly affects equines. The symptoms include:
- Snotty nose
- Yellowish pus from the nose
- Dry Cough

If the broodmare is affected, it will damage or kill the fetus. If a young foal is affected, he may develop pneumonia and may even die.

Prevention
- Every 6 months, have all donkeys that are under the age of 5 vaccinated.
- In the 5th, 7th and 9th month of pregnancy, all broodmares should be vaccinated.

Potomac horse virus
This is a condition that occurs when the animal ingests insects like mayflies, dragonflies, damselflies, stoneflies, snails or larvae of these insects. The common symptoms are:
- Lack of appetite
- Depression
- Dehydration
- Colic
- Diarrhea

If the horse is not vaccinated, he may succumb to the infection.

Prevention
- Vaccinate the animal every year
- Do not let the animal drink from lakes or ponds
- The water troughs and buckets should be kept clean
- During seasons when there are several insects flying about, make sure you turn the lights off at night.
- Make sure that there are no dead insects in the food or water of the donkey.

Equine Viral Arteritis
This disease is very common in donkeys that are breeding. If you are using methods like artificial insemination, the animal is still at risk of developing this condition.

Prevention:
- Any stallion that is going to be bred should be checked 28 days before the breeding season.
- Only clean mares should be bred.
- In the case of artificial insemination, the semen should be tested, especially when it has been imported.
- Vaccinate breeding stallions and mares annually.

If the mare is vaccinated, the virus is still being shed from her body. That means they must be quarantined from the mares that are pregnant. A mare must never be vaccinated in the last 2 months of her gestation period. You must also avoid vaccinating a foal that is less than 6 months old.

Rotovirus
This is a disease that is very common in younger foals. If they are not treated in time, the foal may die.

Prevention
- Pregnant mares should be vaccinated in the 9th or 10th month of pregnancy.
- Visitors should be kept away from young foals.
- Make sure that you wash your hands and keep your boots sterilized every time you handle the foal.

Distemper or strangles

A donkey that is affected by this condition will exhibit these symptoms:

- A swollen throat
- Yellow snotty nose
- Cough
- Puss draining in the throat glands.

This condition is not fatal in donkeys if they have been well maintained. The pasture that is used by these animals will remain infected for a long time, however.

Prevention
- Annually vaccinate the donkey.
- A nasal spray vaccination is a must for foals that are about 4 weeks old.
- Incoming horses or donkeys that look sick should be quarantined.
- When you are handling quarantined horses or donkeys and resident donkeys, you need to make sure that you clean and disinfect your clothes and boots.

Botulism
If your donkey has eaten any food that is moldy, rotten or spoilt, they can develop Botulism or food poisoning. It can also be caused when there are insects or other dead organic matter in the food. If your donkey is affected, it may lead to death in 2-3 days.

Prevention
- Make sure that all the food that you give your donkey is free from any rotten spots mold or insects.
- If you are feeding silage or hay bales to the donkey, make sure that it is thoroughly checked.
- Broodmares must be vaccinated for botulism.
- Also get an opinion from your veterinarian about vaccinating foals.

Opossum Disease or Equine Protozoal Myeloencephalitis (EPM)
This is a disease that horses and donkeys develop when they consume opossum feces. It is zootonic disease that can be fatal to horses and donkeys. When the donkey is affected with this condition, the first symptoms are:
- Inability to coordinate between the limbs
- Loss of mobility in the hind limbs.

Prevention

- Keep the pasture clear of any opossums. You can place traps around the area.
- Make sure that the food containers have enough barriers around them.
- Never serve any food that has the slightest traces of feces on it.

Clostridial Enerocolitis
If there is any change in diet or if your donkey has been on antibiotics, this condition can occur. Even if he has been deprived of hay for a very long time, you will see the following symptoms:

- Swollen belly
- Colic pain
- Diarrhea
- Blood in stools.

Prevention
- Any change in feed should be gradual
- Oral probiotics must be administered to foals right after birth.

Adenovirus
This is a disease that is normally seen in newborn foals. It is for the foals to receive the antivirus from the dam. If not it can be very serious. Initially, you will notice simple symptoms like:
- Labored breathing
- Mild cough.

Prevention
- Keeping the living conditions of young foals very clean
- Washing your hands and feet before handling foals.

Pigeon fever
This condition is also known as dry land heavens and dry land strangles due to the following symptoms:
- The midline has draining pus, abscesses and deep sores
- The swelling on the midline resembles the breastbone of a pigeon, leading to this name.

This disease is usually caused when the donkey has any wound, broken skin or mucous membranes. When these wounds are circled by houseflies, the risk is higher.

The condition is most prevalent in the Western parts of the US.

Prevention
- The donkeys that have been infected must be isolated
- The stall and the equipment must be disinfected fully
- Any bio hazardous material or pus must be disposed of
- Make sure you wash your hands every time you handle the infected animal. Also disinfect the boots and garments you had on while handling them.

The diseases that we will discuss in the following section should be immediately reported to your vet. These are diseases that, by law, need to be reported to a State or Federal Veterinarian.

Brucellosis
The first signs of this disease are fistula on the withers. While this disease is not spread by donkeys to humans, they are carried and transferred by sheep, pigs, deer, goats and other domestic cattle.

Prevention
- If there is any cattle that is infected, you must keep it away from the horse
- The pastures must be fenced to prevent the entry of any wild pigs
- In the US, any cattle tested positive for this condition must be euthanized.

Equine infectious anemia (EIA) or Swamp Fever
This is a condition that is mostly transmitted by horse flies, deer flies, saliva, blood, bodily fluids, milk or unsanitary syringes and needles.

Prevention
- An annual Coggins test must be conducted on horses
- If you are showing your donkey, make sure that he is only taken to events where a negative Coggins Test report is mandatory
- All used syringes and needles must be disposed of in a medical waste container
- A horse or donkey that tests positive for this condition may have to be euthanized as per federal laws.

Vesicular stomatitis
This condition affects humans, livestock, donkeys and wild animals. It is usually transmitted by gnats and flies. You can also contract it if you come into contact with the equipment, feeding buckets or saliva of the animals

that have been infected. This condition can be transmitted from donkeys to humans.

Prevention
- Keep a check on insects
- Maintain individual feeders if possible
- Incoming or imported horses must be quarantined
- Horses that seem sick must be isolated
- When you handle these donkeys, make sure that you have latex gloves on as well as rubber boots. Disinfect them after you handle them and ensure that you change your clothes and thoroughly wash your hands before you handle healthy horses.

African horse sickness
This condition is prevalent in Africa. It is usually transmitted by mosquito bites. There are three forms of this sickness that display this range of symptoms:
- High fever
- Depression
- Cough
- Frothy discharge from the mouth and nostrils
- Troubled breathing
- Swelling in the neck and head
- Pink eye
- Pain

Prevention
- Consult the veterinarian about the potential of exposure in your area and also about necessary vaccinations.
- Any horse or donkey that is being imported from Africa must be quarantined for at least 2 months and then tested.

Contagious Equine Meritis
This condition is acute and highly contagious. It is very prevalent in European countries. The stallions are usually carriers that will show no symptoms. The mares, on the other hand, can show several symptoms including:
- Bleeding from the vulva
- Milky pus after about 14 days of breeding
- Failed impregnation
- Abortion

Prevention
- Any filly that has been imported must be quarantined and checked
- If a donkey has tested positive for CEM, you must not breed them until they are treated and declared "clean"
- Hygiene is of utmost importance when you are handling these donkeys
- Disinfect instruments and use disposable gloves when you handle them
- If you suspect this condition in any of your horses, call the vet immediately.

Anthrax
This is a common condition with any cattle that grazes. If you come into contact with an infected animal or its products, you stand the risk of being infected too.

The condition is spread when healthy animals come into contact with the nasal discharge of infected animals or consume contaminated food and grass.

The donkeys that develop this condition show the following symptoms:
- Swollen areas on the neck, belly and throat
- Chills
- Stupor
- Bleeding from the rectum
- Fast breathing
- Staggering
- Coma

It can be fatal to your horses and donkeys.

Prevention
- Before the seasonal outbreaks of anthrax, have your donkey vaccinated. You can consult your vet for this cycle.

Piroplasmosis
A donkey will develop this condition when he is infected by a tick bite or by a reused needle. The infected animal will display these symptoms:
- Weakness
- Loss of appetite about one to two weeks after exposure
- Fever
- Anemia
- Yellowish coloration in the eyes and mouth

- Anemia
- Reddish urine

Prevention
- All used needles and syringes should be disposed correctly
- Ticks should be controlled
- Remove and destroy all ticks from the infected animal
- If a horse or donkey is tested positive for this condition, keep him quarantined at least 300 feet away from the healthy animals
- Return the animal from quarantine only after he has been fully cleared of all the ticks on his body
- Never use syringes that have been used before.

The above-mentioned diseases will affect most equines. If you have a mixed stable, make sure that you have all of the animals tested and vaccinated regularly.

Hypercalcemia
This condition is life threatening in donkeys. When fat reserves are mobilized, they are sent to the liver where they are converted into energy yielding glucose. The issue with donkeys is that they are not great at stopping this mechanism and with time, the liver and kidney degenerate.

Decreased appetite is one of the only signs that the donkey will display when he is hyperccalcemic. There are some conditions that lead to this disease:

- Obesity: If the fat reserves are high, insulin is resisted. You need to monitor the diet of your donkey and watch the weight very carefully.

- Age and gender: The older donkeys are at a greater risk of this condition and so are the mares.

- In the case of late pregnancy or late lactation.

- Diseases like Laminitis and Cushing's disease can lead to this condition.

- Other common factors are surgery, stress or any concurrent disease.

Prevention
- Remove any condition that is causing stress.

- Exercise

Fluid therapy and dedicated care can reduce the symptoms caused by this condition in your donkey. You must keep a regular check on the diet of your donkey after he has been diagnosed with this condition.

Hoof and foot problems

The hooves of a donkey are elastic, small, upright and tough. It is very common for donkeys to develop issues with respect to their hooves. However, with proper care, you can reduce the occurrence of this condition.

Genetically, donkeys are used to living in arid conditions. So, in countries like Europe where the levels of moisture are high, it is common for the donkey to develop foot abscesses, weakness in the walls of the hoof and also thrush. You will have to provide them with constant care to prevent these issues.

Laminitis is one of the most common foot problems in donkeys. It is common in donkeys that eat too much lush or frosty grass. You have to make sure that your donkey gets high fiber and low sugar foods in order to prevent this condition.

Prevention:
- Provide dry bedding
- Ensure the stable is clean
- Fields should be well drained
- Trim the feet every two months to keep them in the best condition.

With these precautions, you can avoid problems that can even lead to lameness and decreased mobility in your pet.

3. Dealing with injuries

When your donkeys are free ranging on the ranch, there are chances that they will have injuries from time to time. You can treat the small bruises and wounds at home. However, when it comes to the larger and deeper wounds, it is best that you consult your vet.

a. Have a first aid kit ready

The first thing that you need to do is to keep a first aid kit handy on the pasture. You will need to have the following items in your donkey first aid kit:

- Cotton wool
- Gauze swabs
- Animal lintex poultice material
- Equine cleansing or antiseptic solution
- Latex gloves
- Thermometer
- Vet's number
- Record of vaccinations

With these items in place, you will be able to treat the wounds of your animal quite easily. Make sure that you replace used items at the earliest.

b. First steps to treating a wound
- Make sure you prevent further injury.

- Catch the donkey and make sure you can calm him down. If your donkey is frightened you need to also stay aware of your own safety.

- Examine the wounds thoroughly. If you are examining the wound on the feet, be additionally cautious.

- In the case of minor wounds, clean the wound up first with clean and cold water. This step helps control bleeding and also ensures that there is no swelling.

- The wound should be fully cleansed using a gauze pad. The antiseptic solution must be diluted as per the instructions on the pack.

- If there is any hair in the region around the wound, make sure that you cut it off carefully to prevent any contamination of the wound.

- Sprays and powders must never be used unless you have been advised to do so by your veterinary surgeon. These may push the dirt deeper into the wounds.

If you have any doubts about the wound being infected, make sure that you consult your vet. Keep an eye out for any unpleasant smell or discharge on the wound. After you remove the bandage, you have to keep examining the wounds.

When the wounds are healing, they may cause some discomfort to your donkey. This will lead to self-trauma in the form of itching, rubbing or biting the wounded area. You can ask your veterinary surgeon for assistance in this case.

In the case of serious injuries, you will have to cover it with gauze and apply pressure to prevent bleeding. If the blood seeps through the gauze that you apply, do not remove it. Instead, just add a second layer on it to keep the bleeding under control.

c. When should you call the vet?
You must call your vet if you notice one or more of the following:

- Bleeding is excessive. If there is any wound on the lower legs, it will bleed profusely. Make sure you apply enough pressure on it with gauze before you call your vet.

- If the wound has punctured through the thick skin of the donkey.

- If the wound is close to the joint.

- If the wound is below knee level or if it is severe.

- If the wound has been contaminated by dirt or any other material.

- If you notice inflammation, lumps, swelling or bruising without obvious signs of a wound, it can be a warning sign of other underlying health issues in the donkey.

4. Dealing with broken bones
Just as in the case of the horse, a broken bone in a donkey is also enough cause for concern. There are several reasons why your donkey may have a broken bone:

- He might have fallen when walking or trotting

- It could be from a fight with another donkey. One violent kick is enough to break a donkey's bones.

- Micro fractures are caused due to wear and tear caused from the nature of work that the donkeys do on your pasture. This can heal if the donkey is given time to recover.

- Chip fractures are common in donkeys and are usually due to orthopedic conditions. These chips are usually seen in the hock joint, fetlock and the knee of the donkey.

Diagnosis of fractures

There are a few obvious signs of a fracture in a donkey. This is what you need to look out for:

- You will actually hear the popping sound if you are around when the injury occurs. This is followed by swelling and pain in that region.

- Inability to walk.

- Inability to apply any pressure on the area that is injured.

- Wincing or moving away when you try to touch that area.

Treating fractures

In most of the hairline and micro fractures, rest is the only way to help the animal recover. This is successful in most cases.

However, in the case of serious fractures, a screw is used to keep the bones in place. Specially designed steel equine screws can be used for the donkey. Screws can be placed permanently or may be removed after the fracture has healed.

The removal of these screws depends entirely upon the degree to which the wound has healed and also the severity of the actual injury.

Plates can also be used in the case of fractures in donkeys. These plates are usually removed in younger donkeys that will have to continue to work on farms and pastures. However, if the donkey is old and can retire after the injury, then the plate is removed.

If the plate needs to be removed, it means that the donkey will have to undergo another surgery. Of course, there is a lot of new technology in equine surgery such as bio-absorbable screws or titanium screws. They are expensive but they will prevent surgery.

In most cases, a cast is placed if the only option is rest for the donkey to recover. This includes a very light supportive bandage that is placed directly over the affected area.

4. Donkey dental care

Any pain or discomfort in your donkey's teeth can lead to negative behavior. Usually any change in the donkey's behavior is due to bad equipment and the former. Many times people use discipline techniques when the real problem is associated with the health of the animal, particularly the condition of his teeth.

Now, teeth in equines push up against the jaw constantly. They will wear with grazing eventually. Therefore, a hole or decay is not cause for concern, as it will wear out in time. There are several other problems that may occur in the teeth or the mouth that require good treatment. It is best that you have the teeth of your donkey checked regularly because, most often than not, it can lead to several other problems.

a. Signs of dental issues
- Sudden loss in body condition.
- Severe eating disorders. The donkey will not be able to chew well or eat properly.
- You will notice undigested foods in the stool of the animal.
- There will be recurring digestive issues like colic pain.
- The donkey will have foul breath.
- Constant head tossing shows that his teeth may be digging into the noseband.
- He will drool or foam at the mouth.
- You may notice discharge from one side of the nostril.

The discharge in the nostril is usually the result of an abscess or broken tooth that has become infected. This condition is quite serious and can lead to infections that will spread to the sinus cavity. Your equine may have to undergo surgery in order to solve this issue to prevent any infections in the other parts of the body.

Usually, the incisors will never cause any issues. These are the nipper teeth in the front. The grinding teeth, or the molars, are the ones that cause a lot of issues. They will wear and tear unevenly leading to several problems for the donkey. They may form sharp edges that will cut the cheeks and also the tongue of the animal. This can be corrected by a process called floating where all the sharp edges are rasped. This process is not painful and donkeys will be comfortable with it.

The most common dental issues are:
- **Teeth shedding:** The caps or the deciduous teeth will remain on permanent teeth sometimes, leading to an uneven chewing surface.

This also leads to a lot of food getting trapped in the teeth, leading to inflammation from the spiking jaw. For this, you will have to pull the caps out.

- **Missing teeth:** If the teeth do not have a surface that can grind opposite them, they will pinch into the hole. This can be extremely painful for the animal.

- **Wolf teeth:** In most equines, the first premolars or the wolf teeth are missing. This is not the canine that is seen in the males. They will be seen in the upper jaw just in front of the grinding teeth. These are small formations but extremely sharp. The donkey will be irritated by it. You can have these teeth removed by an equine dentist. If you are confident about handling the donkey, you can also check this by inserting your finger in the space between the incisors and the molars. You will feel the presence of this tooth there.

- **Bolus:** If there is a lump of un-chewed food in the cheeks, it will cause inflammation and must be removed at the earliest.

- **Mouth abscesses:** This is seen if any tooth is lodged in the tongue or the mouth. You have to pull the seeds out and have the mouth hosed. This can lead to uneven surfaces that lead to cuts and wounds.

- **Old age:** When donkeys are older, they will need a lot of care. They are most prone to dental issues. The wear and tear in the tooth can lead to blindness and deafness as it leads to poor chewing. When equines are very old, they will wear out. This is when you will have to provide soft food and also vitamins to the animal. The good news, however, is that this wear and tear is a lot better in donkeys, leading to a longer lifespan.

The dental health of equines should never be ignored. If you are suspicious of any problem, you can consult your vet, who should be able to suggest a qualified equine dentist.

5. Finding a good equine vet

Taking care of your donkey means that you need to have him vaccinated regularly and even checked thoroughly every year. For this, you have to find a specialist or an equine vet who can deal with specific health issues related to these animals.

A good equine vet will have these qualities:

- **Good communication:** An equine vet should be able to give you all the options available when it comes to getting your donkey treated. A good vet should be able to tell you how a certain treatment works, what the advantages are and also the alternatives.

    They should be patient enough to explain every treatment process in steps and also describe the possible outcome and the support work that is needed after treatment.

    When you meet the vet for the first time, ask as many questions as you can. If they seem to have the same philosophy in terms of providing care for the donkey, you can build a long lasting relationship.

- **Experience and education:** You need to know all the details such as the area that the vet specializes in, the college that they graduated from and the other details. You need to know how much experience the vet has and how many different kinds of cases they have handled.

    It is best to find a vet who is a part of the American Association of Equine Practitioners.

- **The general character:** The vet should have qualities like the desire to serve when you need them, integrity and of course intelligence. Now, there are other factors like how the vet talks, if they are too chatty or just the general personality. Choose one who will suit your level of comfort.

- **Ability to handle the donkey:** This is the best mark of experience. Now, not all donkeys are easy to handle. If your vet loses his/her cool very easily, then you may not be able to have smooth procedures and check-ups. Some procedures are inherently stressful for a donkey and a good vet will be able to find alternatives to do it thoroughly and easily.

- **Multi vet facility or solo practitioner:** This is an important decision to make. A solo practitioner is preferred by many as they will have the same vet seeing them each time. On the other hand, if you choose a multi vet facility, you will have access to specialists who have more experience.

In a multi vet facility, you will also have access to better technology. The process is a lot more standardized and you will see that it is also a lot more sustainable.

- **Availability:** The biggest downside with solo practitioners is that their availability is limited. However, they can compensate for this with the best after hours management. In any case, you will have to discuss backup and emergency services with your vet.

  You must make availability a priority, as in the case of an emergency that is what will come in handy. You must also be reasonable with expectations. If the vet is handling a more severe case than yours, let them prioritize that case.

- **Check for additional facilities:** It is a good idea to check out all the facilities and surgical equipment available. The better the facilities, the better it is for you. Of course, the equipment is only as good as the handler. So a qualified vet should always be your choice over technology.

- **The specialization:** You must be aware of the specialization of your vet. For instance, you may have an equine only practice as well as a mixed animal practice. It is best that you choose an equine only practice as there is a lot to work on when it comes to donkeys and equines. However, if you are certain that your vet specializes in equines, working with other small species should not be a red flag in any case.

A vet is a very important part of your journey with your donkey. In most cases, the extreme illnesses may not have a positive outcome and you may have to choose drastic measures like euthanizing the donkey. That is when you will need complete support from your vet. In a sense, a confident and sensitive vet will empower you.

When choosing your vet, you need to keep proximity in mind. You should be able to rush your donkey to the vet in an emergency. Even the best equine vet who is too far away is of no use. You can find a qualified Equine vet with the Get-A-DMV feature that is available on the official American Association of Equine Practitioners, www.aaep.org

6. Preventing common illnesses

With most of the common illnesses that your donkey may contract, the end result is always quite drastic and will claim the life of your donkey if not treated at the earliest.

Now, there are a few measures that you can take to control these common issues with your beloved pet:

- **Quarantine all incoming donkeys**: This applies to horses as well. It is necessary to keep the new equine in a separate stable for a few days to observe for the manifestation of any illnesses. If you suspect that your new donkey has the slightest illness, consult your vet. Most often, the new donkey will look absolutely fine in health when he comes to you, but he may be a carrier. Quarantining will give the disease time to manifest.

- **Keep the stable clean**: Make sure that you give your donkey a clean environment to stay in. The stable and all the equipment should be cleaned on a regular basis. If you are handling a quarantined donkey, make sure you wear gloves and rubber shoes that are sanitized. You may also want to change the clothes before handling your resident donkeys.

- **Provide clean food:** If there are any traces of dust, feces or dead insects in some foodstuff, you must never feed it to your donkey. The food containers must be protected from rodents and other pests who may transmit diseases through bodily fluids and their excreta.

- **Keep the pasture free from predators:** Most often, diseases are caused by predators that may leave droppings on grass, bite a donkey or horse or even contaminate food. You can speak to the forest authorities in your area to learn about the common predators in your area. Use appropriate fencing depending upon the type of predator you need to keep at bay.

- **Vaccinate the donkeys regularly:** Most of the fatal and zootonic conditions can be prevented with the appropriate vaccination. Here is a list of the important vaccinations along with their cost annually:

  - Tetanus- $2 $20/ £1- £10
  - EEE- $2 $20/ £1- £10
  - WEE- $2 $20/ £1- £10
  - VEE- $2 $20/ £1- £10

- Rabies- $10- $20/ £5- £10
- West Nile Virus- $35- $45/ £15- £20
- Flu- $5- $50/ £2- £25
- Rhino- $15- $25/ £8- £15
- Botulism- $20- $50/ £10- £25
- Potomac Horse Fever- $25- $40/ £10- £20
- Strangles-$20- $50/ £10- £25

According to the American Association of Equine Practitioners, you have to vaccinate all of the horses and donkeys at your stable for the above illnesses.

7. Getting insurance for your donkey

Treatments for several health issues can be expensive, starting from as high as $2000 or £1500. So it is best that you choose some form of insurance to take care of them, unless you have enough contingency funds in place. Now, most insurance companies that offer pet insurance will have equine insurance that you can claim for the medical expenses of your pet.

Here are some tips to choose the best insurance for your donkey:

- Choose what you want to insure. Some donkey owners will want to have a comprehensive policy while others may choose only specific requirements. The premium that you pay will depend upon what you want the insurance to cover.

- Check the age limit for insuring the donkey. Some policies will require you to insure your pet before it reaches a certain age and will only cover injuries and medical expenses after the donkey reaches a certain age. The insurance may not be valid for senior donkeys in some cases.

- Vet fees are the most important criteria when it comes to insuring your donkey. However, you will have to look at other options like the treatments and procedures that are covered by the policy. For instance, in some cases you may have limits upon the number of times you can claim insurance for procedures like MRI scans. It is very important to choose the insurance based on the conditions, your budget and the things you can claim for.

- Check for insurance policies that cover for third party liability. In case any damage or injury is caused by your pet to people, property or other domestic animals, this will offer complete protection if you are found to be legally responsible.

- You must make sure that the insurance covers any requirement irrespective of whether the donkey is being handled by you, your family and friends or a keeper.

- One important cover offered by equine insurance is permanent loss of use. This is necessary if your donkey is a working animal on your farm. In case an illness or injury renders your donkey incapable of carrying out certain activities on your farm, insurance can be claimed. There is usually an age limit for this claim that is between the age of 2 and 17 years.

- The insurance policy must cover standards like theft, straying and death. In these cases, you can claim the market value unless the sum insured is of lower market value.

- You can opt for a personal accident benefit that will not only cover a rider but also family members, friends and keepers as a standard.

- Getting tack cover and saddle cover is a good idea to help you incase of any theft.

- If your donkey draws a vehicle or a trailer, you can have that insured as well.

If you have more than one donkey, you will also get discounts on the remaining herd. If you have several donkeys in one stable, it is a good idea to have them all insured under the same provider.

8. Understanding equine euthanasia

As your donkey gets older, you may have to deal with the terrible decision of euthanizing the animal. In several cases, physical issues lead to severe mental trauma that can even make your donkey a threat to you and your family.

In most cases, emotions will creep in and you will begin to second-guess this decision. However, it is best that you take the advice of the vet if you are dealing with serious issues with respect to your animal.

Now, there are several signs that will tell you that it is time to let go. Some will be obvious and the others will be a lot more subtle.

a. When to let go

If you see these signs in your equine friend, you must consider euthanasia as an alternative:

- A fracture in the long bone that is meant to bear weight. In most cases, even if the owner has access to funds and medical care, euthanasia is an option if an adult donkey has a broken leg.

- If the tissue in this long bone is broken due to a ruptured ligament, the damage is permanent.

- If the donkey is in a lot of pain, he will exhibit behaviors like self-thrashing, mental disorders and even a loss in equilibrium. These side effects due to pain are not treatable.

- Any external evidence of trauma or shock in the form of gray blue, white or red colored gums, increased heart rate at rest, extremities that are ice cold, mental depression, etc.

- Exposure of abdominal contents due to the improper healing of a surgery site or rupture of a body wall.

- A chronic condition such as difficulty in or excessive eating, urination, drinking and defecation that is not treatable even after repeated medical intervention.

- Any condition that leaves your donkey unable to move, stand or even defend himself.

- Any condition that makes a donkey aloof and disinterested in his companion. This is a sign of caution, as companionship is as important as food to donkeys.

b. Methods of euthanasia
There are several, painless methods that can help put your donkey to rest without causing too much suffering.

Lethal injection

Advantages:

- This is the most humane and quiet method when done correctly.

Disadvantages:

- There are very few barbiturates that will shut the brain down before the rest of the body. Others may lead to suffocation or paralysis.

- Not all vets can provide barbiturates that are licensed.

- If the person injecting the horse does not do it correctly, it will have a very violent reaction.

- Sometimes, the drug may not work on the donkey.

- If a house pet consumes any tissue or blood from the body of the animal euthanized with an injection, it can lead to them slipping into a coma.

Gunshot

Advantages
- This is the most instantaneous and reliable method of euthanizing the animal.

- There is no real danger if other animals come into contact with the body of the deceased donkey.

Disadvantages
- There is a lot of social and emotional stigma attached to it.

- If the person euthanizing the donkey is not skilled, it can be unsafe and also extremely inhumane.

Putting a pet donkey to sleep can be one of the most challenging decisions you will ever take as a pet owner. However, in some cases it is the most humane thing to do in order to ensure that you do not cause further damage to the donkey. You need to make sure that the body of the pet donkey that is euthanized is buried or cremated properly for safety reasons.

Conclusion

Hopefully, you have received a good insight into having a donkey as a pet. It is important for every donkey owner to consider the risk involved in bringing a donkey home.

These animals are extremely powerful and need a competent handler. If you are not experienced, make sure that you gain some information about rearing donkeys before actually investing in one.

Once you are confident about handling donkeys, this book can be a great guide to ensure that you have a wonderful journey with your donkey. It takes a lot of involvement to raise a happy and healthy donkey. But, if you are able to succeed, you will have a fun and fuzzy companion.

References

Learning as much as you can about your donkey can really help you create the best developmental environment for your pet. It is true that donkeys are wonderful companions provided you are able to give them all the care that they need. Here are a few websites that can help you stay updated with all the information you need about a donkey.

Note: at the time of printing, all the websites below were working. As the internet changes rapidly, some sites might no longer be live when you read this book. That is, of course, out of our control.

www.thedonkeysanctuary.org.uk

www.donkeybreedsociety.co.uk

www.livestocktransportblog.com

www.thedonkeysanctuary.ie

www.bioweb.uwlax.edu

www.archaeology.about.com

www.longearsmall.com

www.ed.ac.uk

www.thedancingdonkey.blogspot.in

www.longhopes.org

www.bensonranch.com

www.equinerescuefrance.org

www.forums2.gardenweb.com

www.motherearthnews.com

www.donkeysanctuary.co.za

www.fastonline.org

www.seasidedonkey.co.uk

www.equinenow.com

www.donkeywhispererfarm2010.wordpress.com

www.modernfarmer.com

www.lovelongears.com

www.archaeology.about.com

www.denverpost.com

www.gov.uk

www.quatr.us

http://www.thehorse.com

www.petplanequine.co.uk